An Analytic Theology
of Evangelism

VERITAS
Series Introduction

"The truth will set you free" (John 8:32)

In much contemporary discourse, Pilate's question has been taken to mark the absolute boundary of human thought. Beyond this boundary, it is often suggested, is an intellectual hinterland into which we must not venture. This terrain is an agnosticism of thought: because truth cannot be possessed, it must not be spoken. Thus, it is argued that the defenders of "truth" in our day are often traffickers in ideology, merchants of counterfeits, or anti-liberal. They are, because it is somewhat taken for granted that Nietzsche's word is final: truth is the domain of tyranny.

Is this indeed the case, or might another vision of truth offer itself? The ancient Greeks named the love of wisdom as *philia*, or friendship. The one who would become wise, they argued, would be a "friend of truth." For both philosophy and theology might be conceived as schools in the friendship of truth, as a kind of relation. For like friendship, truth is as much discovered as it is made. If truth is then so elusive, if its domain is *terra incognita*, perhaps this is because it arrives to us—unannounced—as gift, as a person, and not some thing.

The aim of the Veritas book series is to publish incisive and original current scholarly work that inhabits "the between" and "the beyond" of theology and philosophy. These volumes will all share a common aspiration to transcend the institutional divorce in which these two disciplines often find themselves, and to engage questions of pressing concern to both philosophers and theologians in such a way as to reinvigorate both disciplines with a kind of interdisciplinary desire, often so absent in contemporary academe. In a word, these volumes represent collective efforts in the befriending of truth, doing so beyond the simulacra of pretend tolerance, the violent, yet insipid reasoning of liberalism that asks with Pilate, "What is truth?"—expecting a consensus of noncommitment; one that encourages the commodification of the mind, now sedated by the civil service of career, ministered by the frightened patrons of position.

The series will therefore consist of two wings: (1) original monographs; and (2) essay collections on a range of topics in theology and philosophy. The latter will principally be the products of the annual conferences of the Centre of Theology and Philosophy (www.theologyphilosophycentre.co.uk).

Conor Cunningham and Eric Austin Lee, *series editors*

Available from Cascade Books

[Nathan Kerr	Christ, History, and Apocalyptic: The Politics of Christian Mission][1]
Anthony D. Baker	Diagonal Advance: Perfection in Christian Theology
D. C. Schindler	The Perfection of Freedom: Schiller, Schelling, and Hegel between the Ancients and the Moderns
Rustin Brian	Covering Up Luther: How Barth's Christology Challenged the Deus Absconditus that Haunts Modernity
Timothy Stanley	Protestant Metaphysics After Karl Barth and Martin Heidegger
Christopher Ben Simpson	The Truth Is the Way: Kierkegaard's Theologia Viatorum
Richard H. Bell	Wagner's Parsifal: An Appreciation in the Light of His Theological Journey
Antonio Lopez	Gift and the Unity of Being
Toyohiko Kagawa	Cosmic Purpose, translated and introduced by Thomas John Hastings
Nigel Zimmerman	Facing the Other: John Paul II, Levinas, and the Body
Conor Sweeney	Sacramental Presence after Heidegger: Onto-theology, Sacraments, and the Mother's Smile
John Behr et al. (eds.)	The Role of Death in Life: A Multidisciplinary Examination of the Relation between Life and Death
Eric Austin Lee et al. (eds.)	The Resounding Soul: Reflection on the Metaphysics and Vivacity of the Human Person
Orion Edgar	Things Seen and Unseen: The Logic of Incarnation in Merleau-Ponty's Metaphysics of Flesh
Duncan B. Reyburn	Seeing Things as They Are: G. K. Chesterton and the Drama of Meaning
Lyndon Shakespeare	Being the Body of Christ in the Age of Management
Michael V. Di Fuccia	Owen Barfield: Philosophy, Poetry, and Theology
John McNerney	Wealth of Persons: Economics with a Human Face
Norm Klassen	The Fellowship of the Beatific Vision: Chaucer on Overcoming Tyranny and Becoming Ourselves
Donald Wallenfang	Human and Divine Being: A Study of the Theological Anthropology of Edith Stein
Sotiris Mitralexis	Ever-Moving Repose: A Contemporary Reading of Maximus the Confessor's Theory of Time

---

1. Note: Nathan Kerr, Christ, History, and Apocalyptic, although volume 3 of the original SCM Veritas series, is available from Cascade as part of the Theopolitical Visions series.

Sotiris Mitralexis et al. (eds.)	*Maximus the Confessor as a European Philosopher*
Kevin Corrigan	*Love, Friendship, Beauty, and the Good: Plato, Aristotle, and the Later Tradition*
Andrew Brower Latz	*The Social Philosophy of Gillian Rose*
D. C. Schindler	*Love and the Postmodern Predicament: Rediscovering the Real in Beauty, Goodness, and Truth*
Stephen Kampowski	*Embracing Our Finitude: Exercises in a Christian Anthropology between Dependence and Gratitude*
William Desmond	*The Gift of Beauty and the Passion of Being: On the Threshold between the Aesthetic and the Religious*
Charles Péguy	*Notes on Bergson and Descartes*
David Alcalde	*Cosmology without God: The Problematic Theology Inherent in Modern Cosmology*
Benson P. Fraser	*Hide and Seek: The Sacred Art of Indirect Communication*
Philip John Paul Gonzales	*Exorcising Philosophical Modernity: Cyril O'Regan and Christian Discourse after Modernity*
Caitlin Smith Gilson	*Subordinated Ethics: Natural Law and Moral Miscellany in Aquinas and Dostoyevsky*
Michael Dominic Taylor	*The Foundations of Nature: Metaphysics of Gift for an Integral Ecological Ethic*
David W. Opderbeck	*The End of the Law? Law, Theology, and Neuroscience*
Caitlin Smith Gilson	*As It Is in Heaven: Some Christian Questions on the Nature of Paradise*
Andrew T. J. Kaethler	*The Eschatological Person: Alexander Schemann and Joseph Ratzinger in Dialogue*
Emmanuel Falque	*By Way of Obstacles: A Pathway through a Work*
Paul Tyson (ed.)	*Astonishment in Science: Engagements with William Desmond*
Darren Dyk	*Will & Love: Shakespeare and the Motion of the Soul*
Matthew Vest	*Ethics Lost in Modernity: Reflections on Wittgenstein and Bioethics*
Hanna Lucas	*Sensing the Sacred: Recovering a Mystagogical Vision of Knowledge and Salvation*
Philip John Paul Gonzales et al. (eds.)	*Finitude's Wounded Praise: Responses to Jean-Louis Crétien*
Martin Koci et al. (eds.)	*God and Phenomenology: Thinking with Jean-Yves Lacoste*
Steven E. Knepper (ed.)	*A Heart of Flesh: William Desmond and the Bible*

An Analytic Theology of Evangelism

A Classical Theist's Approach

TYLER DALTON MCNABB

CASCADE *Books* • Eugene, Oregon

AN ANALYTIC THEOLOGY OF EVANGELISM
A Classical Theist's Approach

Veritas

Copyright © 2024 Tyler Dalton McNabb. All rights reserved. Except for brief quotations in critical publications or reviews, no part of this book may be reproduced in any manner without prior written permission from the publisher. Write: Permissions, Wipf and Stock Publishers, 199 W. 8th Ave., Suite 3, Eugene, OR 97401.

Cascade Books
An Imprint of Wipf and Stock Publishers
199 W. 8th Ave., Suite 3
Eugene, OR 97401

www.wipfandstock.com

PAPERBACK ISBN: 979-8-3852-0473-1
HARDCOVER ISBN: 979-8-3852-0474-8
EBOOK ISBN: 979-8-3852-0475-5

Cataloguing-in-Publication data:

Names: McNabb, Tyler Dalton, author.
Title: An analytic theology of evangelism : a classical theist's approach / by Tyler Dalton McNabb.
Description: Eugene, OR: Cascade Books, 2024 | Series: Veritas | Includes bibliographical references.
Identifiers: ISBN 979-8-3852-0473-1 (paperback) | ISBN 979-8-3852-0474-8 (hardcover) | ISBN 979-8-3852-0475-5 (ebook)
Subjects: LCSH: Evangelistic work. | Evangelistic work—Philosophy. | Evangelistic work—Ethics.
Classification: BV3793 M360 2024 (paperback) | BV3793 (ebook)

VERSION NUMBER 11/01/24

I dedicate this volume first to my wife, Priscilla, and my six children, Eden, Elijah, Ezra, Eva-Maria, Ezekiel, and Evangeline. Second, I dedicate this volume to Billy Abraham. Memory Eternal, my friend.

Contents

Acknowledgments | xi

A (Very) Short Introduction | 1

Part I: The Gospel
Chapter 1: The Gospel and the Call | 7
Chapter 2: Justification: Catholic and Confessional Protestant Views | 25

Part II: The Model
Chapter 3: A Model from the Saints | 45
Chapter 4: An Analytic Christology of Religions | 57

Part III: The Objections
Chapter 5: Evangelism as Epistemic and Cultural Violence | 81
Chapter 6: It's the End: A Short Reflection on How Many
    Will Be Saved | 91

Appendix: Approaches to Street Evangelism | 97
Bibliography | 99

Acknowledgments

BILLY ABRAHAM SHOWED ME that you can be an analytic scholar and write a book on evangelism. Billy's work was influential to say the least. However, not many have followed his path to produce an analytic work on evangelism. While Billy was alive, I had told him that writing an evangelism book would be my next project. As a young scholar, I had too many projects to keep up with. Unfortunately, I did not pick up the project while Billy was alive. After his passing, however, I knew that I had to become serious about this book and see it to completion. In a sense then, this book would not exist without Billy and his witness.

Of course, the book wouldn't be possible if it weren't for my wife and children. They sacrificed time away from me in order to enable me to write this project. This book in a sense is for them. Of course, there are friends that need to be thanked. Specifically, I want to tell my colleagues at Saint Francis University, Gregory Stacey, Brian Besong, Dan Waldow, and Fr. Stephen Waruszewski, that I appreciate our conversations about evangelism and our time evangelizing together. I'd also like to thank my former colleague, Jerry Walls. Jerry has been excited about this project for many years now. He has been an encouragement for years.

I'd like to thank some contemporary evangelists who have fostered my interest in evangelism. I'd like to thank Ray Comfort and Kirk Cameron whose work originally got me interested in evangelism as I got serious about my faith in the early part of 2007. I'd also like to thank those at St. Paul Street Evangelization, who gave me a Catholic model for evangelism,

ACKNOWLEDGMENTS

once I crossed the Tiber. Finally, I want to thank those who I labored with. I especially want to thank Jeff Rose.

Finally, I'd like to thank the journal *Religions* and my good friend Michael DeVito for allowing me to use the following paper:

> Tyler Dalton McNabb and Michael DeVito, "A Christology of Religions and a Theology of Evangelism," *Religions* 13 (2022) 926.

A (Very) Short Introduction

IN CASE YOU PICKED up the wrong book, let me state the obvious: This book is about evangelism. Now, I know, it is surprising that there is an academic book written on this topic. Outside of Billy Abraham's *The Logic of Evangelism*,[1] Elmer Thiessen's *The Ethics of Evangelism*,[2] and Bryan Stone's *Evangelism After*[3] series, the philosophical literature on evangelism is practically nonexistent. While topics such as Christology, the doctrine of the Trinity, and God's love all deserve attention, it seems as if analytic theologians have completely abandoned any concern for the theology of evangelism. As an analytic philosopher of religion, I've be waiting years for a correction to be made. Sadly, no correction has come. And with my friend Billy Abraham passing away in 2021, I've decided to honor his legacy and concern for evangelism by writing a book to help grow the analytic literature.

Unlike Billy, I am not a Methodist nor a son of one. I am a Catholic who is in good standing with the Bishop of Rome. As such, this book, while written for a "Mere Christian" audience, will at times pay special attention to Catholic theologians and the Catholic tradition. This will seem especially to be the case in chapters 3 and 4. My Protestant brothers and sisters need not worry, however. I will also engage leading Protestant biblical scholars and theologians. However, my engagement at times will

---

1. Abraham, *Logic of Evangelism*.
2. Thiessen, *Ethics of Evangelism*.
3. See, for example, Stone, *Evangelism After Pluralism*.

seem a bit disproportionate. If this is unacceptable, then please, by all means, write your own theology of evangelism. The analytic field will be all the better for it.

As for those who can tolerate my papist concerns, I must confess another unpopular commitment. Contrary to Billy Abraham's wishes, I am what he calls a Neo-Thomist.[4] Not even in the line of Eleanor Stump's much more personalist glossing of Thomas,[5] but in the line of Brian Davies's "God is not a thing" Thomism.[6] I am a Classical Theist of the Davies stripe. Without fully explicating the sort of Thomism that I assume in this book, I'd like to briefly articulate three important theses[7] that I will make reference to in this volume.

First, I will assume that God is immutable. Here I don't have in mind a significantly weaker version of this doctrine where God is immutable in the sense that he will always remain faithful or that God will be just as good today as he will be tomorrow. No. I have in mind the much stronger version of this thesis where God as pure act, lacks utter potential to change in any way.

God being pure act of course, entails the second thesis that I want to explicitly endorse. God is impassible. Once again, while there are weaker versions of this thesis, I have in mind the strongest articulation. Because God lacks potentiality, creatures lack the ability to bring about change in God's action or even his train of thought.

Finally, I'll assume that God is metaphysically simple; that is, God lacks parts. While we talk about God possessing various properties such as being omniscient, omnibenevolent, and omnipotent, in a strict sense, God's omniscience just is his omnibenevolence, and his omnibenevolence just is his omnipotence. In fact, what we predicate to God are really just shorthand descriptions of saying the same thing, namely that God is. God is identical to Existence itself.[8]

Okay. Enough rambling. Hopefully the reader has a clear understanding of this book's assumptions and will be able to draw the right connections when I make reference to the God of Classical Theism. Having

---

4. Abraham, *Divine Agency and Divine Action*.
5. Stump, *Aquinas*.
6. Davies, *Thought of Thomas Aquinas*.
7. For a more robust explication see McNabb and Baldwin, *Classical Theism and Buddhism*.
8. Gilson, *Christian Philosophy of St. Thomas Aquinas*, 29–32.

clarified this, I now move to outline the structure of the book. The book is divided into three sections. Part I contains two chapters. Chapter 1 is primarily aimed toward three things: defining the gospel and the nature of evangelism, arguing for the historicity of the gospel, and arguing that all Christians are called to evangelize. Among many volumes here, I am in indebted to William Abraham's volume *The Logic of God*. I show that there is no disagreement between Catholics and Protestants as it relates to the contents of the gospel. I will draw from both binding Catholic documents and the Evangelical declaration known as the Lausanne Covenant.

Chapter 2 begins where chapter 1 leaves off. Namely, I answer how it is the case that gospel forgives our sins. Specifically, I argue that Catholic and Confessional Protestant accounts of the doctrine of justification are consistent with each other.

The first chapter in Part II (chapter 3) focuses on developing a model for evangelism. I do this first by surveying important evangelists in the past and use their insights to develop a model for evangelism. Evangelists surveyed include the following: Saint Patrick, Saint Francis, Matteo Ricci, George Whitefield, Pope John Paul II, and Billy Graham.

In the final chapter of Part II (chapter 4), I will utilize Vatican II and specifically the work of Gerald O'Collins and Keith Ward to develop a Christology of religions. The theology of religions developed, I argue, should also shape how the church evangelizes non-Christians. Overall, I argue that while Jesus is the only way to God, we should be optimistic about the eternal destiny of non-Christians who die. Non-Christians who die, for all we know, are saved by Christ insofar as they are implicit or (to reference Rahner) anonymous Christians. Moreover, I argue that many traditional religions can be interpreted to be logically consistent with the doctrines of Christianity. Because of this, I argue that the evangelist should be less concerned with philosophical arguments against other religions, and more concerned with showing how Christ's claims are consistent with the relevant non-Christian religious tradition.

Finally, in Part III, I engage various objections to evangelism. First, in chapter 5, I argue against the claim that evangelism is immoral. Reasons for thinking evangelism is immoral include the following: evangelism is a form of colonialism and thus leads to cultural destruction, and, evangelism is inherently manipulative. Finally, I will specifically address Samuel Lebens's recent argument against evangelism.[9] In the final

---

9. Lebens, "Proselytism as Epistemic Violence."

chapter, chapter 6, I reflect on how many will be saved and whether our answer to this question should influence the level of urgency we have in our evangelistic efforts.

My hope in all this is simple. I want to give a theology of evangelism, defend its practice, and develop a model for evangelizing the nations. Whether the book is successful in doing all of this remains to be seen. If this book fails with respect to these desires, I will at least succeed in publishing something on the topic of evangelism from an analytic perspective. Sadly, merely publishing on the topic is indeed a noteworthy contribution. Regardless, I pray that this book will serve as a catalyst to spark many more scholarly discussions on the topic of evangelism. And that this will, in turn, spark a revival in Christendom.

Part I

The Gospel

1

The Gospel and the Call

THIS BOOK IS ABOUT evangelism. But what exactly is evangelism? Whatever evangelism is, it includes sharing the gospel. No, I'm not talking about sharing all of Matthew, Mark, Luke, or John. By gospel, here, I mean the rule of faith for the early church. Irenaeus articulates the early rule of faith by stating the following:

> For the Church, though dispersed throughout the whole world, even to the ends of the earth, has received from the apostles and their disciples this faith: in one God, the Father Almighty, who made the heaven and the earth and the seas and all things that are in them; and in one Christ Jesus, the Son of God, who became incarnate for our salvation; and in the Holy Spirit, who proclaimed through the prophets the dispensations and the advents, and the birth from a virgin, and the passion, and the resurrection from the dead, and the incarnate ascension into heaven of the beloved Christ Jesus, our Lord, and his future manifestation from heaven in the glory of the Father to sum up all things and to raise up anew all flesh of the whole human race in order that . . . he should execute just judgement towards all; that he may send spiritual wickednesses, and the angels who transgressed and came into a state of rebellion together with the ungodly, and unrighteous, and wicked, and profane among men, into the everlasting fire; but may, as an act of Grace, confer immortality on the righteous and holy, and those who have kept his commandments, and have persevered in

his love, some from the beginning, and others from their repentance, and may surround them with everlasting glory.[1]

What is essential to the rule of faith, specifically as it pertains to our salvation? Why is it that 'the Son of God . . . became incarnate for our salvation'? We can dig deeper into these questions by seeing how the gospel was preached by the apostles. In Acts 2:22–41, we see Peter give more details as to how the incarnation saves humanity:

> [22] "Men of Israel, hear these words: Jesus of Nazareth, a man attested to you by God with mighty works and wonders and signs that God did through him in your midst, as you yourselves know— [23] this Jesus, delivered up according to the definite plan and foreknowledge of God, you crucified and killed by the hands of lawless men. [24] God raised him up, loosing the pangs of death, because it was not possible for him to be held by it. [25] For David says concerning him,
>
> 'I saw the Lord always before me,
>   for he is at my right hand that I may not be shaken;
>
> [26] therefore my heart was glad, and my tongue rejoiced;
>   my flesh also will dwell in hope.
>
> [27] For you will not abandon my soul to Hades,
>   or let your Holy One see corruption.
>
> [28] You have made known to me the paths of life;
>   you will make me full of gladness with your presence.'
>
> [29] "Brothers, I may say to you with confidence about the patriarch David that he both died and was buried, and his tomb is with us to this day. [30] Being therefore a prophet, and knowing that God had sworn with an oath to him that he would set one of his descendants on his throne, [31] he foresaw and spoke about the resurrection of the Christ, that he was not abandoned to Hades, nor did his flesh see corruption. [32] This Jesus God raised up, and of that we all are witnesses. [33] Being therefore exalted at the right hand of God, and having received from the Father the promise of the Holy Spirit, he has poured out this that you yourselves are seeing and hearing. [34] For David did not ascend into the heavens, but he himself says,
>
> "'The Lord said to my Lord,
>
> "Sit at my right hand,

---

1. Irenaeus, *Against the Heresies* 1.10.1, 111–12.

> ³⁵ until I make your enemies your footstool.'"
>
> ³⁶ Let all the house of Israel therefore know for certain that God has made him both Lord and Christ, this Jesus whom you crucified."
>
> ³⁷ Now when they heard this they were cut to the heart, and said to Peter and the rest of the apostles, "Brothers, what shall we do?" ³⁸ And Peter said to them, "Repent and be baptized every one of you in the name of Jesus Christ for the forgiveness of your sins, and you will receive the gift of the Holy Spirit. ³⁹ For the promise is for you and for your children and for all who are far off, everyone whom the Lord our God calls to himself." ⁴⁰ And with many other words he bore witness and continued to exhort them, saying, "Save yourselves from this crooked generation." ⁴¹ So those who received his word were baptized, and there were added that day about three thousand souls.[2]

Peter's audience is told that they have sinned by killing God's anointed. Nonetheless, Peter references the Psalms to argue that God would not let his "Holy One see corruption." While Jesus was "delivered up according to the definite plan and foreknowledge of God . . . God raised him up." In fact, Jesus now sits at the "right hand" of God. Peter finishes his sermon by declaring that those who repent and are baptized in the name of Jesus will have their sins forgiven and will be granted the gift of the Holy Spirit. According to Peter, then, there is something to Jesus' foreordained death and resurrection that forgives sins.

Paul, likewise, explains that the incarnation saves humanity through the death and resurrection of the Son of God. In his letter to the Corinthians, Paul exhorts his readers to hold on to the "gospel" that he preached to them, lest they "believed in vain." Paul then goes on to define this message:

> Now I would remind you, brothers, of the gospel I preached to you, which you received, in which you stand, ² and by which you are being saved, if you hold fast to the word I preached to you— unless you believed in vain.
>
> ³ For I delivered to you as of first importance what I also received: that Christ died for our sins in accordance with the Scriptures, ⁴ that he was buried, that he was raised on the third day in accordance with the Scriptures, ⁵ and that he appeared to Cephas, then to the twelve. ⁶ Then he appeared to more than five hundred brothers at one time, most of whom are still alive, though some

---

2. Unless further stipulated, Bible references are from the English Standard Version.

> have fallen asleep. ⁷ Then he appeared to James, then to all the apostles. ⁸ Last of all, as to one untimely born, he appeared also to me. ⁹ For I am the least of the apostles, unworthy to be called an apostle, because I persecuted the church of God. ¹⁰ But by the grace of God I am what I am, and his grace toward me was not in vain. On the contrary, I worked harder than any of them, though it was not I, but the grace of God that is with me. ¹¹ Whether then it was I or they, so we preach and so you believed. (1 Cor 15:1–11)

It is interesting to note that Paul's definition of the gospel likely does not originate with Paul. Most scholars believe that Paul's list of those who the resurrected Christ appeared to is an early creed of the church that dates back to the first few years after the death of Christ.³ Nonetheless, Paul is clearly approving of the message. Paul tells us that the gospel is defined in the following way: "Christ died for our sins in accordance with the Scriptures, that he was buried, that he was raised on the third day in accordance with the Scriptures," and that he appeared to the apostles. The heart of the gospel is in reference to the death and resurrection of the Christ.

Now, in Mark 1:14–15, we famously read the following: "Now after John was arrested, Jesus came into Galilee, proclaiming the gospel of God, and saying, 'The time is fulfilled, and the kingdom of God is at hand; repent and believe in the gospel.'" How is it then that Christ, before his death, burial, and resurrection, preached the gospel? A key feature of the gospel that is often neglected is the context for the good news. Even after returning from the Babylonian captivity, Israel was in a sense still in exile. Israel was waiting for God's presence to be greater in the second temple than it was in the first temple (Hag 2:9). While being granted some autonomy, Israel was still captive to occupation, this time Roman occupation. The sick, disabled, and hungry were still ever present. Israel yearned for the establishment of God's kingdom. Jesus comes on to the scene and explains to Israel that the eschatological kingdom was here. Jesus heals the sick and feeds the hungry, which are all a manifestation of God's kingdom. Jesus even informs John the Baptist that he is fulfilling the messianic expectations expressed in Suffering Servant passages in Isaiah. Jesus preached that the kingdom was being inaugurated and the messianic age was near. The message of the apostles (i.e., the death, burial, and resurrection of the Son of God) exists within this wider kingdom message. That is, it is through the death, burial, and resurrection of Christ, that healing, restoration, liberation, and salvation take place.

---

3. Licona, *Resurrection of Jesus*, 223–35.

Pope John Paul II puts it this way:

> Jesus of Nazareth brings God's plan to fulfillment. After receiving the Holy Spirit at his Baptism, Jesus makes clear his messianic calling: he goes about Galilee "preaching the Gospel of God and saying: 'The time is fulfilled, and the kingdom of God is at hand; repent and believe in the Gospel'" (Mk 1:14–15; cf. Mt 4:17; Lk 4:43). The proclamation and establishment of God's kingdom are the purpose of his mission: "I was sent for this purpose" (Lk 4:43). But that is not all. Jesus himself is the "Good News," as he declares at the very beginning of his mission in the synagogue at Nazareth, when he applies to himself the words of Isaiah about the Anointed One sent by the Spirit of the Lord (cf. Lk 4;14–21). Since the "Good News" is Christ, there is an identity between the message and the messenger, between saying, doing and being. His power, the secret of the effectiveness of his actions, lies in his total identification with the message he announces; he proclaims the "Good News" not just by what he says or does, but by what he is.[4]

We can then articulate the gospel as follows:

> Central Gospel Message (CGM): God grants humanity entrance into his kingdom, and thus forgiveness of sins, through the death, burial, and resurrection of his Son, King Jesus, as it was promised in Israel's Scriptures.

Notice here that Catholics and Protestants, *contra* some Reformed hot takes, do not disagree on the gospel. No confessional Protestant or Catholic would deny CGM. There is complete, I repeat, complete agreement on the gospel message. For further evidence of this claim, we can see how recent popes have defined the gospel message and contrast it with how leading Protestant theologians define it.

Pope Paul VI summarizes the gospel message as follows:

> As the kernel and center of His Good News, Christ proclaims salvation, this great gift of God which is liberation from everything that oppresses man but which is above all liberation from sin and the Evil One, in the joy of knowing God and being known by Him, of seeing Him, and of being given over to Him. All of this is begun during the life of Christ and definitively accomplished by His death and resurrection.[5]

---

4. Pope John Paul II, *Redemptoris Missio*.
5. Pope Paul VI, *Evangelii Nuntiandi*.

PART I: THE GOSPEL

Pope Francis, in his *Evangelii Gaudium*, reaffirms Pope Paul's account of the gospel in more than one place. Below, Francis argues that speaking about death and resurrection of Christ is the first proclamation in evangelism:

> In catechesis too, we have rediscovered the fundamental role of the first announcement or kerygma, which needs to be the centre of all evangelizing activity and all efforts at Church renewal. The kerygma is trinitarian. The fire of the Spirit is given in the form of tongues and leads us to believe in Jesus Christ who, by his death and resurrection, reveals and communicates to us the Father's infinite mercy. On the lips of the catechist the first proclamation must ring out over and over: "Jesus Christ loves you; he gave his life to save you; and now he is living at your side every day to enlighten, strengthen and free you." This first proclamation is called "first" not because it exists at the beginning and can then be forgotten or replaced by other more important things. It is first in a qualitative sense because it is the principal proclamation, the one which we must hear again and again in different ways, the one which we must announce one way or another throughout the process of catechesis, at every level and moment.[6]

The Catholic Church isn't alone in summarizing the Gospel in this way. The Evangelical manifesto on evangelism, the *Lausanne Covenant*, defines evangelism (i.e., announcing the gospel) as follows:

> To evangelize is to spread the good news that Jesus Christ died for our sins and was raised from the dead according to the Scriptures, and that, as the reigning Lord, he now offers the forgiveness of sins and the liberating gifts of the Spirit to all who repent and believe. Our Christian presence in the world is indispensable to evangelism, and so is that kind of dialogue whose purpose is to listen sensitively in order to understand. But evangelism itself is the proclamation of the historical, biblical Christ as Saviour and Lord, with a view to persuading people to come to him personally and so be reconciled to God. In issuing the gospel invitation we have no liberty to conceal the cost of discipleship. Jesus still calls all who would follow him to deny themselves, take up their cross, and identify themselves with his new community. The results of evangelism include obedience to Christ, incorporation into his Church and responsible service in the world.[7]

---

6. Pope Francis, *Evangelii Gaudium*.
7. Lausanne Community for World Evangelization, *Lausanne Covenant*.

THE GOSPEL AND THE CALL

Anglican theologian N. T. Wright's glosses the gospel in kingdom language when he states the following:

> The Gospel is the royal announcement that the crucified and risen Jesus, who died for our sins and rose again according to the Scriptures, has been enthroned as the true Lord of the world. When this Gospel is preached, God calls people to salvation, out of sheer grace, leading them to repentance and faith in Jesus Christ as the risen Lord.[8]

John Dickson and Michael Bird are even more explicit:

> The Gospel is the announcement that God has revealed his kingdom and opened it up to sinners through the birth, teaching, miracles, death and resurrection of the Lord Jesus Christ, who will one day return to overthrow evil and consummate the kingdom for eternity.[9]

> The Gospel is the announcement that God's kingdom has come in the life, death, and resurrection of Jesus of Nazareth, the Lord and Messiah, in fulfillment of Israel's Scriptures.[10]

Having clarified what we mean by the gospel, we can bring clarity to what we mean by evangelism more generally. William Abraham argues that we should consider the process of evangelism as "that set of intentional activities which is governed by the goal of initiating people into the kingdom of God for the first time."[11] For Abraham, evangelism relates to initiating nonbelievers into the kingdom of God. While proclamation is a necessary feature to evangelism, teaching the newcomer the basics of the faith, kingdom ethics, and spiritual discipline are all part of the process of evangelism. Any process that is aimed toward initiating a subject into the life of the church is evangelism.

Pope John Paul and Pope Paul are in agreement with Abraham. Evangelization of course consists of preaching the death, burial, and resurrection of Jesus, but it also consists of much more.

> To be truly a people at the service of life we must propose these truths constantly and courageously from the very first proclamation of the Gospel, and thereafter in catechesis, in the various

---

8. Cited in Wax, "Justification Debate," 34–35.
9. Dickson, *Best Kept Secret of Christian Mission*, 22.
10. Bird, *Evangelical Theology*, Kindle loc. 995.
11. Abraham, *Logic of Evangelism*, 95.

forms of preaching, in personal dialogue and in all educational activity. Teachers, catechists and theologians have the task of emphasizing the anthropological reasons upon which respect for every human life is based. In this way, by making the newness of the Gospel of life shine forth, we can also help everyone discover in the light of reason and of personal experience how the Christian message fully reveals what man is and the meaning of his being and existence. We shall find important points of contact and dialogue also with non-believers, in our common commitment to the establishment of a new culture of life.[12]

In fact the proclamation only reaches full development when it is listened to, accepted and assimilated, and when it arouses a genuine adherence in the one who has thus received it. An adherence to the truths which the Lord in His mercy has revealed; still more, an adherence to a program of life—a life henceforth transformed—which He proposes. In a word, adherence to the kingdom, that is to say, to the "new world," to the new state of things, to the new manner of being, of living, of living in community, which the Gospel inaugurates.[13]

Once again, Catholic theology of evangelism and Protestant theology of evangelism are in sync. Of course, there might be disagreement with respect to how one enters into union with Christ and there could be disagreement as to what theory best explains how one's sins are forgiven, but that discussion is for the following chapter. As for now, what we have done is argued that Catholics and Protestants are on the same page when it comes to defining the gospel and the process of evangelizing. Moreover, I have given a succinct account of the gospel that the rest of this book will assume. I want to now argue for two propositions:

(P1) Assuming that theism is true, the gospel message is historically plausible.

(P2) All baptized persons, at least in normative situations, are called to share the gospel message.

I first move to argue for (P1).

---

12. Pope John Paul II, *Evangelium Vitae*.
13. Pope Paul VI, *Evangelii Nuntiandi*.

Historical Jesus Studies

In ancient historical inquiry, it is common to, at least at times, appeal to various criteria to make a case that some event happened.[14] Here are two that are used that we will make use of:

> Criterion of Multiple Attestation (CMA): If event E is claimed to have occurred in multiple independent sources, then there is some justification for thinking that E occurred.
>
> Criterion of Embarrassment (CE): If a subject S conveys that an event E has occurred, and, E is embarrassing to S and/or S's community, if S has nothing to gain by conveying E, then there is some justification for thinking that E occurred.

The following are facts that most New Testament historians affirm:

> Fact 1: Jesus died by crucifixion.
>
> Fact 2: Jesus was buried in a tomb.
>
> Fact 3: The tomb became empty.
>
> Fact 4: The disciples sincerely believed that they had encountered the risen Jesus.
>
> Fact 5: Saul, a persecutor of the early church, claimed to have encountered the risen Jesus.[15]

Utilizing CMA, we easily see why (F1) is plausible. The Gospels testify to Jesus' death by crucifixion. As discussed earlier, the early creed behind Paul's definition of the gospel in 1 Cor 15:3 confirms Jesus' death. Elsewhere, Paul, and Peter, among others, testify to this claim. If Q is a source, then there is yet another independent source testifying to this claim. Finally, Josephus[16] and Tacitus[17] both reference this event.

Regarding (F2) and (F3), these facts can be made plausible by (CE). The early church's archnemesis was the Sanhedrin. Generally, one doesn't typically say or do things that make their enemies look good. And yet, that

---

14. Michael Licona for example, argues that classicists such as Anke Ronholz use the criteria of embarrassment. See Licona, "Is the Sky Falling in the World of Historical Jesus Research?"; cf. Ronholz, "Crossing the Rubicon," 440.

15. See Habermas, *On the Resurrection Evidences*, 1009–15.

16. Josephus, *Antiquities of the Jews*, Book 18, Chapter 3.

17. Tacitus, *Annals* 15:44.

is exactly what we see when we read the claim that Joseph of Arimathea buried the body of Jesus in a tomb. If you are making up an account of someone burying Jesus, why associate the burial with an enemy? Why not someone like Zacchaeus or a Roman centurion? Dale Allison wonders why make up a name at all. As he puts it,

> [W]hy bother to recall his name? Would they have done so had he merely thrown Jesus into a burial plot for criminals, or if he had treated Jesus the way other criminals were treated? The Gospels are full of nameless characters. Matti Kankaaniemi has a point when he infers that something "unexpected in Joseph's act inspired Jesus' followers to mention his name." Kankaaniemi then observes, "private burial by a Sanhedrinist matches well with the 'unexpected.'"[18]

Moreover, unfortunately, women's testimony was not taken seriously in first-century Israel.[19] And yet, who do the Gospels mention were the first to see the empty tomb? The women. In fact, the embarrassing nature of women's testimony may be why Paul leaves the women out in 1 Corinthians 15 and why Luke removes the women's resurrection encounter altogether. If you are trying to start a religious movement in first-century Israel, best leave out that women were the first to see the empty tomb.

With respect to (F4), there is some evidence to suggest that the disciples sincerely believed that they had encountered the risen Jesus. Sean McDowell has argued extensively that we can have moderate confidence that several members of the twelve died martyr's deaths.[20] It is one thing to die for a belief that you think is true but it turns out to be false. It is a whole other thing to die for some proposition you know is false. The disciples testified that they had encountered the risen Jesus even to the point of great suffering. (F4) then seems plausible. Of course, in addition to this, we also see that there are early traditions testifying to the fact that the disciples had encountered the risen Jesus (e.g., 1 Corinthians 15:3).

Finally, (F5) is claimed in Paul's own epistles. There is overwhelming consensus that Paul, even in his uncontested authentic letters, sincerely believes this. We see once again, that Paul believes that his encounter was veridical to the point where he was willing to suffer imprisonment and ultimately, death.

18. Allison, *Resurrection of Jesus*, 194.
19. Josephus, *Antiquities of the Jews*, 4:219.
20. McDowell, *Fate of the Apostles*.

So, how can we make sense of (F1–F5)? One standard explanation of these facts is what is called the hallucination hypothesis. Roughly, the idea is that the disciples sincerely believed that Jesus was the Messiah. Seeing their messiah die in a cursed way caused cognitive dissonance. This ended up resulting in the disciples hallucinating the risen Christ. Similarly, Saul, having persecuted the early church, felt guilt, and could no longer handle his pain of having harmed others. Paul, likewise, hallucinates the risen Jesus.

While this might seem initially plausible, it does not explain (F3). One will need an additional hypothesis to explain (F3) away. Of course, postulating more and more hypotheses creates more and more room for error. It would be better to endorse a simpler hypothesis that could cover all the facts. Moreover, we see from 1 Corinthians 15 that there was an early testimony that the disciples had encountered the risen Jesus together. The Gospels seem to have a memory of the twelve (at that time, the remaining eleven) experiencing the risen Jesus as a group. And yet, there is almost nothing written on group hallucinations in the peer review psychology literature. Hallucinations generally only happen with one of the senses as well. While it is true that the parapsychology literature does discuss group hallucinations, again, this is generally a rare phenomenon. It seems implausible then, though not impossible, that the disciples hallucinated as a group, and Paul hallucinated independently. If God's existence is already in one's background knowledge (k), the explanation that God raised Jesus from the dead seems like a much more viable hypothesis.

More recently, however, the aforementioned criteria has come under attack. Some New Testament historians have argued that we should do away with the traditional criteria.[21] Esteemed New Testament scholar Dale Allison, for example, argues that all the criteria are "fatally flawed" and "not strong enough to resist our wills."[22] Rafeal Rodriguez takes a look at various supposedly "embarrassing" texts found in the Gospels, and argues that the criterion of embarrassment can't deliver historical validation. For example, typically it has been argued that Jesus' baptism was an embarrassment to the early Christian community. After all, why is someone sinless being baptized? The tradition of Jesus' baptism must have some authenticity. Not so fast, Rodriguez argues. Using the works of various critics to the criterion, Rodriguez argues that the supernatural elements of the text

21. Keith and Le Donne, *Jesus, Criteria, and the Demise of Authenticity*.
22. Allison, *Historical Christ and the Theological Jesus*, 53–78.

PART I: THE GOSPEL

(e.g., the Spirit descending like a dove and the Father audibly speaking) could point to the text being a later theological reflection rather than a memory of the historical Jesus. Moreover, following Leif Vaage, Rodriguez argues that the embarrassing elements of the passage can be explained away simply by understanding that this is an instance where the Christian community is attempting to communicate the upside-down effects of the Gospel where those who become last are first and those who are first are really last.[23] Rodriguez goes on to look at other "embarrassing" passages and argues that it might be the case that what looks to be embarrassing to us was not actually embarrassing to the early Christians.[24] For example, while Rodriguez isn't personally persuaded that the early Christians invented to story that Jesus was being accused of being demon possessed, he admits there could be good reason for doing this.

It's not just the criterion of embarrassment that has come under attack. As already noted, even the criterion of multiple attestation has recently taken hits. The standard objection goes something like this: Multiple attestations of some particular event would indeed up the likelihood that the event really happened, but how can we verify that the sources involved are actually independent? For example, maybe Tacitus is using Josephus to confirm the historical Jesus, and perhaps Josephus is using sources from Paul to discuss the crucifixion of Jesus. How can we tell if our "independent" sources are really independent after all?

In place of the criteria, New Testament historians have turned to memory studies to support their quest for the historical Jesus. For example, Robert McIver uses various case studies to argue for the position that big picture memory is reliable. McIver references John Yuille and Judith Cutshall's study of a deadly robbery that took place three months prior to their receiving details about the case.[25] Yuille and Cutshall grilled eyewitnesses of the robbery and found that 80 percent of the details given were accurate. The 20 percent that were not accurate did not impede on overarching or central details of what happened.[26]

McIver then looks specifically at the reliability of group memory. Using the works of Baumeister and Hastings and Barry Schwartz, McIver argues that while contemporary collective "memory" of individuals

---

23. Rodriguez, "Criteria of Embarrassment," 142.
24. Rodriguez, "Criteria of Embarrassment," 142–43.
25. McIver, "Collected Memory and the Reliability of the Gospel Tradition," 131.
26. McIver, "Collected Memory and the Reliability of the Gospel Tradition," 131–32.

THE GOSPEL AND THE CALL

or events can be remade to fit the purposes of a certain agenda or the spirit of the age, the historical reinvention of the individual or event is still bound by historical record.[27] For example, we may forget that Abe Lincoln wanted to send former slaves back to Africa, but we still recall a general truth that Abraham Lincoln abolished slavery in the states. Similarly, we may forget to what extent the Soviets contributed to destroying Nazi Germany and we might overexaggerate America's and Britain's role in World War II, but the gist of what happened is still in our collective memory.[28] As Allison states it, "Eyewitnesses may disagree on the details of a car wreck, but all agree that there was one."[29]

The paradigm view in New Testament studies is that the Gospels are what you call Greco-Roman biographies. They are biographies in the sense that they convey the history of a person. However, the ancient genre of biographies can differ from today's biographies. For example, today chronology is vital to the success of a well-researched biography. In ancient biographies, chronology takes a back seat to conveying a larger point about a person or event. Similarly, today biographies are judged by how accurate the statements given by an individual are. Ancient biographies are okay with paraphrasing speeches and even attributing speeches to individuals that the individual would likely communicate.[30]

Nonetheless, ancient biographies are still biographies and they attempt to convey truth about an individual based on memories of the community. The Gospels appear to be full of eyewitness testimony and early sources. Luke for example opens up his Gospel by saying the following:

> Inasmuch as many have undertaken to compile a narrative of the things that have been accomplished among us, 2 just as those who from the beginning were eyewitnesses and ministers of the word have delivered them to us, 3 it seemed good to me also, having followed all things closely for some time past, to write an orderly account for you, most excellent Theophilus, 4 that you may have certainty concerning the things you have been taught. (Luke 1:1–4)

Anthony Giambrone, in his *A Quest for the Historical Christ*, asks his reader if Luke was a lying historian.[31] Essentially, if you think Luke is being an

27. McIver, "Collected Memory and the Reliability of the Gospel Tradition," 142–43.
28. McIver, "Collected Memory and the Reliability of the Gospel Tradition," 143.
29. Allison, *Historical Christ*, 61.
30. Licona, *Why Are There Differences in the Gospels?*
31. Giambrone, *Quest for the Historical Christ*, 88–91.

honest historian, then the Gospel records testimony from those who claim to be eyewitnesses to the life of Christ. Of course, if you think Luke is lying for his agenda, then much of what he says can be discarded. Using the principle of charity, it seems like we should trust Luke until given reason to not trust him. As far as we are concerned then, it is plausible that Luke contains at least some eyewitness testimony.

Richard Bauckham gives us additional reasons for thinking that the Gospels contain memory that can be traced back to eyewitnesses. Bauckham postulates that at least in some cases, when you see a name mentioned in the Gospels that explains a familial relation, the name plausibly can connect us to eyewitness testimony. For example, in Mark, we read that Simon of Cyrene helps Jesus pick up his cross. We are told that Simon is the father of Alexander and Rufus. Mark going out of his way to explain that Simon of Cyrene is the father of Alexander and Rufus demands an explanation. One explanation for why Alexander and Rufus are mentioned is that the sons of Simon are the source for the story in question. Moreover, Alexander and Rufus would likely be names that the early communities would recognize, showing that Mark's Gospel was written to an audience within a living life span of Jesus.[32] It seems, then, that the Gospels contain reliable testimony.

More to the point, if the Gospels are Greco-Roman biographies, there is an attempt to convey truth by the author. As Allison argues, the more some theme or event is mentioned, the more likely it is that there is a historical truth behind the theme or event.[33] For example, if we see multiple instances of Jesus preaching an apocalyptic sermon, while we can't guarantee the sermon's contents from a historical perspective, there probably is some truth behind these sermons such as Jesus was an apocalyptic preacher. Similarly, if we see Jesus battling Satan in the wilderness and casting out demons in his ministry, we can say that Jesus was probably known for his opposition to demonic forces. Again, big picture memory is reliable. We can then see if the big picture depiction of Jesus is consistent with first-century Judaism as well as see how this depiction fits with the early church's beliefs, and conclude some modest facts about the historical person of Jesus.[34] While I agree with Allison that the criteria don't force us to historical

---

32. Bauckham, *Jesus and the Eyewitnesses*, 52.
33. Allison, *Constructing Jesus*.
34. This is the same methodology Michael Barber uses in his *Historical Jesus and the Temple*.

conclusions "against our wills," I think some of the rejection of the criteria has been too hasty.

For example, while there are cases where it isn't clear if two sources are independent, there are some cases that seem to be independent from one another. For example, I doubt many give serious consideration that Tacitus's source for the death of Christus is the same source as the early creed found in 1 Corinthians 15:3. Of course, we can be skeptical about whether sources are truly independent. It can't be ruled out as an impossibility. But it also can't be ruled out as an impossibility that we are in a simulation right now that is similar to the Matrix (of the film by that name). If we apply this level of skepticism to history or to just about anything else, we lose knowledge. But surely we have knowledge, including historical knowledge.

Similarly, I think the field has been too hasty with respect to rejecting the criterion of embarrassment. Daniel Wallace argues that we can trace what was seen as embarrassing to the early church by way of reading textual variants. We can see how scribes changed or altered various texts when the texts came in tension with their theology.[35]

Fernando Bermejo-Rubio argues that the Gospels have gone through a depoliticization process. That is, the Gospels try to deemphasize to what extent Jesus was a revolutionary or political leader. Nonetheless, Bermejo-Rubio argues that one can see echoes of the revolutionary image of Jesus in the Gospels. For example, Jesus tells his disciples to pick up their cross and follow him, he instructs for his disciples to die with him, he has a political triumphal entry, he claims that his kingdom is arriving imminently, and he informs his disciples to buy two swords. These references, taken together with the number of troops mentioned in the Gospels that were sent to arrest Jesus, all point to a political Jesus. These are leftover artifacts that portray Jesus as a political revolutionary.[36] The Gospel writers for obvious reasons want to deemphasize the political Jesus while emphasizing a more spiritual and heavenly-minded Jesus. These "leftovers" are embarrassing to the Gospel writers, and yet are still mentioned. This leads Bermejo-Rubio to argue that we can in fact locate what is embarrassing to the Gospel authors and gain a plausible understanding of the historical Jesus from this investigation. Bermejo-Rubio's larger point is that while we can try to explain why some event mentioned in the Gospels might not be so embarrassing after all, at least if we look at the text atomistically,

---

35. Wallace, "Textual Criticism and the Criterion of Embarrassment," 123–24.
36. Bermejo-Rubio, "Changing Methods, Disturbing Material," 13–14.

when we take various seemingly embarrassing events together, we can recognize an overall pattern that leads us to identify embarrassing facts about Jesus and the early church.

All this to say, if we utilize the traditional criteria with the understanding that we can't obtain historical certainty about the historical Jesus and we utilize such traditional criteria in conjunction with Allison's aforementioned methodology, I think use of the traditional criteria can be justified. For example, thanks to Paul and Luke, we can recognize a pattern that the women's encounter with Jesus and his empty tomb is embarrassing. We can also see that the empty tomb narrative is repeated in all four Gospels. This would meet Allison's repetition criteria. Moreover, we see that the tomb being empty fits perfectly with what we know about eschatological resurrection according to first-century Jewish thought. The tomb would need to be empty if one's body is, eschatologically speaking, glorified. And finally, the empty tomb explains the early church's belief in Jesus. Utilizing all of these points lead us to the conclusion that plausibly there was an empty tomb.

All Are Called

Having now defended (P1), I move to arguing for (P2). For my Catholic audience, I could merely recite papal encyclicals to make plausible my claim. For example, Pope Paul IV is clear that all Christians are called to witness and evangelize:

> The command to the Twelve to go out and proclaim the Good News is also valid for all Christians, though in a different way . . . All Christians are called to this witness, and in this way they can be real evangelizers. We are thinking especially of the responsibility incumbent on immigrants in the country that receives them.[37]

But why do they think this? Surely my Protestant readers might demand that I give scriptural support for this claim. Of course, the most cited passage supporting the view that are baptized Christians should evangelize is Matthew 28:16-20:

> 16 Now the eleven disciples went to Galilee, to the mountain to which Jesus had directed them. 17 And when they saw him they worshiped him, but some doubted. 18 And Jesus came and said to them, "All authority in heaven and on earth has been given to me.

---

37. Pope Paul VI, *Evangelii Nuntiandi*.

19 Go therefore and make disciples of all nations, baptizing them in the name of the Father and of the Son and of the Holy Spirit, 20 teaching them to observe all that I have commanded you. And behold, I am with you always, to the end of the age."

Now, one might argue that the Great Commission was only given to the apostles or perhaps those in charge of the church. Instead of seeing this as a general call for those baptized to aid in initiating unbelievers into the rule of Christ, Matthew 28 is simply calling those in authority (i.e., pastors) to evangelize. This was a commandment given to the apostles; it wasn't a commandment spoken to a more general audience. If one is inclined to interpret Matthew 28 in this way, one might also be sympathetic to endorsing what I call Those In Authority Thesis (TAT). TAT advocates argue that only pastors have obligations to evangelize. This thesis contrasts with the All Are Called Thesis (AAC). Which thesis should we prefer?

Of course, we can look at the Gospels and see that post-resurrection, the women were the first evangelists (Matt 28:8–9), even though the women weren't pastors. We also see that in the book of Acts there were Christians who lacked pastoral authority and yet evangelized. Aquila and Priscilla are a paradigmatic example of this. Moreover, we can look to the early church's witness and see that non-pastors preached the gospel, even to the point of death.[38]

The early church didn't seem to think that evangelism was only the duty of those in charge. Nonetheless, we needn't rely on their witness to see that TAT has to be false. We can develop clear moral counterexamples to TAT such as the following:

> Patrick is a faithful Christian. Patrick goes to church regularly, prays on a daily basis, and donates his time to help feed the poor in his church. Patrick is walking home one day and he runs into a female named Ireland. Ireland, who has been told she has weeks to live, is distraught about what will happen to her after she dies. As Patrick sees her in agony, he decides to ignore her and move on to his nightly activity.

Is Patrick wrong in this scenario? It seems obvious that he is. Patrick has morally failed to do something he ought to have done. Patrick should have done some action that could have helped Ireland become a believer. It is not just that Patrick didn't go above and beyond what he had to do, he had a duty to help Ireland. In this case, it seems obvious that Patrick

---

38. For example, see Justin Martyr's life and work.

has a duty to evangelize even though he is not a pastor of any kind. TAT is then false. Of course, you can change up the scenario to where Patrick has to rush home to save his own children from drowning and, in such cases, Patrick does not have an obligation to evangelize Ireland. But all things being equal, Patrick has a duty.

Now, we can change the scenario such that Ireland does not approach Patrick to discuss her agony. Nonetheless, Patrick knows that there is a real possibility that people around him are in a similar situation as to the one Ireland is in. Does Patrick have an obligation to be intentional and find people who need saving? It seems so.

Let's say that instead of knowing the secret for how man can be reconciled with God, Patrick has a cure that will heal people from a deadly plague that is going around. Patrick doesn't know who has the relevant disease. But it still seems right that Patrick has an obligation to be intentional to find out who needs his cure. It would be wrong if Patrick just sat on his cure unless someone specifically asked him about it. Of course, this doesn't mean that Patrick ought to neglect his work, family, and community in order to go out to find people who need the cure. If Patrick has a family, he plausibly first has obligations to his family before anyone else. Nonetheless, it seems that Patrick should intentionally bring up his cure in conversations he has with people, at least at times. It might not be clear to what extent Patrick should do this, but if Patrick makes no effort to get the news out about his cure, he should be considered selfish. If this all seems right to you, then I think we have a plausible case for ACC. Having made a case for ACC, I move to discuss how it is that the gospel redeems sinners.

2

Justification: Catholic and Confessional Protestant Views

Having now explicated the gospel in broad strokes, and, having argued that in normative contexts, all Christians are obligated to evangelize, I move to bring further elucidation in addressing the particulars of how the death and resurrection of Christ makes us right with God. Notice, I am separating theories of justification from the gospel itself. The gospel is broad and unspecified. And because of this, it seems rather obvious that Catholics and Protestants affirm the same gospel message. Of course, there will be tension with respect to how persons are justified. In this chapter, I argue, *contra* the standard view, that Catholic and many historical Protestant confessions are logically consistent with one another.

Now, one might wonder why I am interested in Confessional Protestantism. I could simply argue that non-Confessional Protestants are not tied to any theory of justification. Assuming the interpretation can be supported in Scripture, the non-Confessional Protestant can endorse the view. In this way, I'd simply have to show why Scripture supports a view that is consistent with Catholic theology. In some ways, this would make things easier. For example, I take it that one can find articulations of justification in the so-called New Perspective on Paul literature that are broadly consistent with Catholic theology.[1] If there is biblical support for

---

1. For one New Perspective that coheres significantly with the Catholic view, see Wright, *Paul and the Faithfulness of God*. On this view, Paul's warnings against relying

PART I: THE GOSPEL

the relevant theory of justification (which I think there is), my job is done. Instead, I want to engage what appears to be a harder puzzle to solve. How can Protestant confessions be made consistent with Catholic teaching? These confessions after all, were written to reflect Reformational theology (i.e., antithetical theology).

Justification

Here is a charactered glossing of how justification works on the Reformed Protestant paradigm (RPP).

> John has sinned before God. John and God are now at odds with one another since John is not righteous and is guilty before God (i.e., a just judge). God the Son, however, becomes man and lives a righteous and obedient life to the Father, to the point such that, qua his human nature, God the Son dies for the sins of the world. This loving action pleases God the Father such that not only does God raise His Son from the dead, but for any subject, S, who ties themselves to Jesus' righteousness, they will receive credit for Jesus' righteousness as if they were actually righteous. That is, S is credited with a foreign righteousness that is not S's own. Since John aligns himself with Jesus, God sees John as righteous. John is therefore reconciled to God.

Notice, here I'm not committing the Reformed Protestant to any theory of atonement, outside of a general substitutionary theory. Nor am I committing the Reformed Protestant to any theory of eschatological justification.[2] Nonetheless, what is key is that S is made righteous before God due to a foreign righteousness being imputed to her. This can be contrasted with a standard Catholic perspective (CP).

> Thomas has sinned before God. Thomas and God are now at odds with one another since Thomas is not righteous and is guilty before God (i.e., a just judge). God the Son, however, becomes man and

---

on the "works of the law" (Gal 2:16) relate to not relying on one's works *per se*, but rather relying on the Mosaic covenant, especially the ceremonial laws that signify the covenant (i.e., circumcision). Here, a subject is initially declared justified (1 Cor 6:11) in the sense that she is declared as a member of the covenant community. One, then, is judged by their works in a final judgement (Rom 2:13; 1 Cor 4:4), but these works (i.e., faithfulness to the covenant) are ultimately grounded in Christ.

2. For different Protestant perspectives on eschatological justification, see Stanley, ed., *Four Views on Works at the Final Judgement*.

lives a righteous and obedient life to the Father, to the point such that, qua his human nature, God the Son dies for the sins of the world. This loving action performed by the Son pleases God the Father such that the Father raises the Son from the dead. However, Thomas needs to become actually righteous before God. Through the normative means of the sacraments, God makes Thomas righteous by infusing into Thomas Christ's righteousness. Christ now lives in Thomas. Since Thomas actually becomes righteous, Thomas is reconciled to God.

I have not mentioned the role that faith plays in initially becoming right with God, nor have I mentioned the source behind one's eschatological justification. Nonetheless, this seems to represent the gist of a standard Catholic conception of the justification process. Having now characterized the RPP and the CP, I move to actually analyze what the confessions of these traditions actually endorse.

Reformed Protestant Confessions

Where shall we start? Let's first look at the 39 Articles of classical Anglicanism.[3] Now, one might object to calling the 39 Articles Reformed in the sense that they do not necessarily endorse a view of predestination. Here, by "Reformed," I just mean a Protestant tradition that finds its origin in the Reformation. It's a broad term that is consistent with the theology of the Five Articles of the Remonstrants. With respect to the doctrine of justification, the 39 Articles state the following:

> XI: We are accounted righteous before God, only for the merit of our Lord and Saviour Jesus Christ by Faith, and not for our own works or deservings. Wherefore, that we are justified by Faith only, is a most wholesome Doctrine, and very full of comfort, as more largely is expressed in the Homily of Justification.

Notice the article on justification does not state anything directly about the doctrine of imputation. The article is rather minimalistic in its elucidation of the doctrine. Of course, we do read that we are only accounted righteous before God because of the merit of Christ, but there isn't a Catholic in the world who would disagree with this. Maybe what is in tension with the Catholic view is the idea that we are justified by faith alone.

---

3. The 39 Articles can be found at the Anglican Communion's website, https://www.anglicancommunion.org/media/109014/Thirty-Nine-Articles-of-Religion.pdf.

Surely this is at odds with Catholic teaching, specifically Canon 9 of Trent, which states the following:

> Canon 9. If anyone says that the sinner is justified by faith alone, meaning that nothing else is required to cooperate in order to obtain the grace of justification, and that it is not in any way necessary that he be prepared and disposed by the action of his own will, let him be anathema.[4]

Anyone who immediately concludes that Canon 9 is inconsistent with Article XI is moving too hastily. Catholics traditionally have interpreted faith as a supernatural virtue that is infused into a subject. The supernatural virtue is specifically related to propositional assent.[5] When Protestants discuss faith, typically what is assumed is something like supernatural trust. For Catholic theology, trust is represented by faith, hope, and charity. What's being rejected here is that one can have saving faith without having hope and love in their heart. This is why Pope Benedict famously stated, "Luther's expression sola fide is true if faith is not opposed to charity, to love."[6] These comments originally surprised many Protestants. But if one reads Trent carefully, the view expressed by Benedict was cemented long before he existed. Canon 11 states the following:

> If any one saith, that men are justified, either by the sole imputation of the justice of Christ, or by the sole remission of sins, to the exclusion of the grace and the charity which is poured forth in their hearts by the Holy Ghost, and is inherent in them; or even that the grace, whereby we are justified, is only the favour of God; let him be anathema.

Notice, what is being condemned here is not the doctrine of imputation, but that one can have full remission of sin without love being poured fourth into one's heart by the Spirit. Faith must always be accompanied by love if that faith is saving.

So, perhaps the statement on faith alone isn't necessarily inconsistent with Trent. The 39 Articles reference the Homily on Justification for a further explication of the Anglican view. Maybe it's there where the real tension between Catholic and Anglican theories of justification exist.

---

4. The Council of Trent's Sessions and Decrees are taken from the following: http://www.thecounciloftrent.com/.

5. McNabb, "Analytic Catholic Epistemologies of Faith: A Survey of Developments."

6. Pope Benedict, *Wednesday Audience*.

The Homily on Salvation clarifies that by "faith alone" one does not mean faith that is alone:

> Nevertheless, this sentence, that we be justified by faith only, is not so meant of them, that they said justifying faith is alone in man, without true repentance, hope, charity, dread, and the fear of GOD, at any time and season. Nor when they say, That we be justified freely, they mean not that we should or might afterward be idle, and that nothing should be required on our parts afterward: Neither they mean not so to be justified without good works, that we should do no good works at all, like as shall be more expressed at large hereafter. But this saying, That we be justified by faith only, freely and without works, is spoken for to take away clearly all merit of our works, as being unable to deserve our justification at GODS hands, and thereby most plainly to express the weakness of man, and the goodness of GOD, the great infirmity of our selves, and the might and power of GOD, the imperfectness of our own works, and the most abundant grace of our Savior Christ, and therefore wholly to ascribe the merit and deserving of our justification unto Christ only, and his most precious blood shedding.[7]

It seems plausible that what is being condemned in the homily is that human beings, from their good works, cannot get right with God. Rather, what gets one right with God are the merits of Christ. Notice, again, that nothing is mentioned about imputation.

But why can't the Catholic agree with all of this? The Catholic Catechism confirms that we are saved by the merits of Christ:

> 1992 Justification has been merited for us by the Passion of Christ who offered himself on the cross as a living victim, holy and pleasing to God, and whose blood has become the instrument of atonement for the sins of all men. Justification is conferred in Baptism, the sacrament of faith. It conforms us to the righteousness of God, who makes us inwardly just by the power of his mercy. Its purpose is the glory of God and of Christ, and the gift of eternal life . . . The grace of Christ is the gratuitous gift that God makes to us of his own life, infused by the Holy Spirit into our soul to heal it of sin and to sanctify it.

There is nothing here about our good works initiating justification. The grace of Christ is "a gratuitous gift." Our justification is achieved by the Passion of Christ. While it is true that Catholics draw distinctions between

---

7. Lancashire, *Homilies*.

PART I: THE GOSPEL

initial justification and final or eschatological justification, as do New Perspective advocates, it is important to point out that while Scripture speaks of our final justification being based on works (e.g., Matt 25:31–46,), the Catholic Catechism is also clear that ultimately our works have supernatural origins: "The charity of Christ is the source in us of all our merits before God. Grace, by uniting us to Christ in active love, ensures the supernatural quality of our acts and consequently their merit before God and before men. The saints have always had a lively awareness that their merits were pure grace." This isn't Pelagianism or semi-Pelagianism. Far from it. The Catholic teaching on justification is pure grace.

Maybe the article on justification is consistent with Catholic teaching. But there are other places in the 39 Articles that reference the doctrine of justification. For example, Article XXXI states:

> The Offering of Christ once made is that perfect redemption, propitiation, and satisfaction, for all the sins of the whole world, both original and actual; and there is none other satisfaction for sin, but that alone. Wherefore the sacrifices of Masses, in the which it was commonly said, that the Priest did offer Christ for the quick and the dead, to have remission of pain or guilt, were blasphemous fables, and dangerous deceits.

Is Article XXI inconsistent with Catholic theology? Catholic teaching is such that one becomes more righteous, or just, as one partakes in the sacraments. The Church teaches that one of those sacraments is the Holy Eucharist. While this isn't the time or place to give an analytic analysis of the doctrine of transubstantiation, we can easily clarify that the Catholic doctrine on the Eucharist does not consist of offering Christ over and over again, as Article XXXI suggests. Hebrews is clear: Christ was sacrificed once and for all (Heb 7:23–28). The Catholic Catechism confirms this as it calls the Eucharist a re-presentation of Christ (CC: 1348). Since Article XXXI seems to be addressing popular views within English Catholicism rather than Trent, it seems like the condemnation it makes does not relate to official Church teaching. John Henry Newman, before his conversion to Catholicism, argued as much:

> Nothing can show more clearly than this passage that the Articles are not written against the creed of the Roman Church, but against actual existing errors in it, whether taken into its system or not. Here the sacrifice of the Mass is not spoken of, in which the special question of doctrine should be introduced; but "the

> sacrifice of masses," certain observances, for the most part private and solitary, which the writers of the Articles knew to have been in force in time past, and saw before their eyes, and which involved certain opinions and a certain teaching . . . That the "blasphemous fable" is the teaching that masses are sacrifices for sin distinct from the sacrifice of CHRIST'S death, is plain from the first sentence of the Article. "The offering of CHRIST once made, is that perfect redemption, propitiation, and satisfaction for all the sins of the whole world, both original and actual. And there is none other satisfaction for sin, but that alone. Wherefore the sacrifice of masses, &c." It is observable too that the heading of the Article runs, "Of the one oblation of CHRIST finished upon the cross," which interprets the drift of the statement contained in it about masses. On the whole, then, it is conceived that the Article before us neither speaks against the Mass in itself, nor against its being [an offering, though commemorative,] for the quick and the dead for the remission of sin; [(especially since the decree of Trent says, that "the fruits of the Bloody Oblation are through this most abundantly obtained; so far is the latter from detracting in any way from the former;")] but against its being viewed, on the one hand, as independent of or distinct from the Sacrifice on the Cross, which is blasphemy; and, on the other, its being directed to the emolument of those to whom it pertains to celebrate it, which is imposture in addition.[8]

One possible response to my use of Newman and my interpretation of the 39 Articles thus far, is that Newman, and myself included, have not done justice to the Anglican tradition. Alister McGrath accuses Newman of using non-mainstream Anglican theologians to help make plausible his interpretations. If Newman looked at the most respected and influential Anglican theologians at the time of the British Reformation, Newman would see that his approach to the 39 Articles would be ruled out. McGrath thinks Newman promotes certain minority theological opinions and passes them off as mainstream to further his own agenda.[9] How should Newman respond?

It seems to me that McGrath thinks Newman should approach the 39 Articles as a legal originalist in the vein of the late American Justice Antonin Scalia. That is, we should look at how the 39 Articles were formulated, who the primary contributors were, and how the early audience interpreted and received the articles. Since it's rather obvious that the

---

8. Newman, *Tracts for the Times*.
9. McGrath, *Iustitia Dei*, 299.

Articles were formulated and interpreted to be in tension with Catholic belief, we should therefore think that the 39 Articles are in tension with Catholic doctrine. This is so even if there are consistently Catholic ways of interpreting the 39 Articles.

But should Newman endorse originalism when it comes to interpreting the 39 Articles? When it comes to Holy Scriptures, traditionally Christians haven't taken an originalist approach. For example, in response to the Marcion controversy, Christians, especially of the Alexandria school, thought to interpret the Old Testament allegorically. This hermeneutic is of course beyond the scope of the original authors and their intentions.

To a lesser extent, Newman could believe that God has made it such that Protestant Confessions of Faith would remain ambiguous on important matters, so that eventual reconciliation and healing would be possible.[10] Another way to put this point: God could make sure that important truths survived the Reformation such that, even if the original authors intended to speak error, truth is preserved so that future generations could reconcile via common ground. This of course doesn't rule out God allowing errors to creep into these confessions, nonetheless, if God had safeguarded the process of these confessions in a broad and general sense, one might expect ambiguity and room for interpreting the Protestant Confession in a way that is consistent with Catholic dogma. No need to be a methodological naturalist. Given that God in some sense causes the Protestant Confessions to exist, and given that he providentially made it such that broad consistency can be established, we can interpret the 39 Articles in the way Newman and I see fit.

In summary, we have seen there is no mention of imputation in the 39 Articles or the Homily on Salvation. We have seen that there are ways of understanding the 39 Articles that are consistent with Catholic theology. Having done this much, I want to look at other Reformed Confessions of Faith.

The 1st London Baptist Confession of Faith states the following:

> XXVIII. Those that have union with Christ, are justified from all their sins by the blood of Christ, which justification is a gracious and full acquittance of a guilty sinner from all sin, by God, through the satisfaction that Christ hath made by His death for all their sins, and this applied (in manifestation of it) through faith.[11]

10. Thanks is owed to Gregory Stacey for talking this through with me.

11. *The First London Baptist Confession of Faith (1646),* https://www.nobts.edu/baptist-center-theology/confessions/First_London_Baptist_Confession_of_Faith_1646.pdf.

Once again, there is no mention of imputation. There isn't even a statement that we are saved by faith alone. The statement on justification is extremely minimalistic. We are told that justification is the result of a gracious full acquittance of the guilt of a sinner through Christ's sacrifice. Of course, nothing here is at odds with the Council of Trent or the Catholic Catechism. Moreover, nothing here is at odds with the 39 Articles.

Much has been written on Lutheran and Catholic perspectives on justification and whether they are reconcilable. Before I give a brief comment on the Joint Declaration, I want to simply point out that the Augsburg Confession, like the other confessions already discussed, has a minimal statement on justification:

> Also they teach that men cannot be justified before God by their own strength, merits, or works, but are freely justified for Christ's sake, through faith, when they believe that they are received into favor, and that their sins are forgiven for Christ's sake, who, by His death, has made satisfaction for our sins. This faith God imputes for righteousness in His sight.[12]

Once again, this Protestant Confession rejects that human beings can get "right" with God through their own merits or works. One is able to identify with Christ's death and the satisfaction Christ brought about through faith. We are told that God imputes faith for righteousness. This is the first time in our survey where we see "imputes." It isn't exactly clear what the word "imputes" is doing here, though it is interesting to see that faith is what is imputed, not directly the righteousness of Christ. Rather, this faith seems to be what grants us righteousness in the sight of God. Once again, there is nothing necessarily inconsistent here with Trent as I've articulated it.

Now, one might argue that if we simply read Melanchthon's work,[13] the author of the confession, we'd see that Philip Melanchthon doesn't mean that God reckons righteousness to the sinner merely because she has faith, but faith is the means God imputes Christ's righteousness. Once again, we must ask ourselves, should we be originalists? Or should we read the document for what it says and see God's providence for what is left out? I'm going with the latter.

In 1999, the Pontifical Council for Promoting Christian Unity and the Lutheran World Federation released a document with the intention

---

12. Krauth, *Augsburg Confession of Faith With a Historical Introduction and Notes*.
13. Melanchthon, *Apology of the Augsburg Confession*.

PART I: THE GOSPEL

to show that their ecclesiastical communions "are now able to articulate a common understanding of our justification by God's grace through faith in Christ." Specifically, both the Catholic Church and the Lutheran Federation signed off on the following:

> By grace alone, in faith in Christ's saving work and not because of any merit on our part, we are accepted by God and receive the Holy Spirit, who renews our hearts while equipping and calling us to good works.[14]

As the Joint Declaration puts it, "The understanding of the doctrine of justification set forth in this Declaration shows that a consensus in basic truths of the doctrine of justification exists between Lutherans and Catholics."[15] Of course, more traditional Lutherans are less pleased about this document. What role does imputation play in the doctrine of justification? Doesn't Trent condemn the doctrine of imputation? Recall that Canon 11 of Trent condemns that men are justified "by the sole imputation of the justice of Christ." The Council doesn't reject imputation wholesale. So, even for Lutherans who see positive imputation as fundamental to the doctrine of justification, there is still room for consistency.

Having now looked at Reformed Confessions, spanning over Anglican, Lutheran, and Baptist traditions, I now move to look at the tradition that *prima facie* seems most at odds with the Catholic theology of justification, high Presbyterian theology. The Westminster Confession of faith states the following:

> Those whom God effectually calleth, He also freely justifieth: not by infusing righteousness into them, but by pardoning their sins, and by accounting and accepting their persons as righteous; not for any thing wrought in them, or done by them, but for Christ's sake alone; not by imputing faith itself, the act of believing, or any other evangelical obedience to them, as their righteousness; but by imputing the obedience and satisfaction of Christ unto them, they receiving and resting on Him and His righteousness by faith; which faith they have not of themselves, it is the gift of God. Faith, thus receiving and resting on Christ and His righteousness, is the alone instrument of justification; yet is it not alone in the person

---

14. Lutheran World Federation, *Joint Declaration on the Doctrine of Justification*, https://www.lutheranworld.org/resources/publication-joint-declaration-doctrine-justification, 31.

15. Lutheran World Federation, *Joint Declaration on the Doctrine of Justification*, 19.

justified, but is ever accompanied with all other saving graces, and is no dead faith, but worketh by love.[16]

Here we have the clearest articulation of the traditional Reformed doctrine of imputation. It is not faith that accounts for our righteousness, but Christ's righteousness. Christ's righteousness is not received through an infusion of grace but rather through pure forensic imputation. Moreover, faith is said to be the *only* instrument that connects us to Christ's righteousness.

Trent, however, suggests differently:

> Of this Justification the causes are these: the final cause indeed is the glory of God and of Jesus Christ, and life everlasting; while the efficient cause is a merciful God who washes and sanctifies gratuitously, signing, and anointing with the holy Spirit of promise, who is the pledge of our inheritance; but the meritorious cause is His most beloved only-begotten, our Lord Jesus Christ, who, when we were enemies, for the exceeding charity wherewith he loved us, merited Justification for us by His most holy Passion on the wood of the cross, and made satisfaction for us unto God the Father; the instrumental cause is the sacrament of baptism, which is the sacrament of faith, without which (faith) no man was ever justified; lastly, the alone formal cause is the justice of God, not that whereby He Himself is just, but that whereby He maketh us just, that, to wit, with which we being endowed by Him, are renewed in the spirit of our mind, and we are not only reputed, but are truly called, and are, just, receiving justice within us, each one according to his own measure, which the Holy Ghost distributes to every one as He wills, and according to each one's proper disposition and co-operation.

We read not that faith is the sole instrument of our justification but rather the sacrament of faith (i.e., baptism) is the instrumental cause of our justification. And there seems to be a clear endorsement that the formal cause of our justification is not imputed righteousness, or both an imputed righteousness and an infused righteousness,[17] but rather that the infused righteousness is the sole formal cause of our justification. Trent ,however, leaves open the possibility that Christ's righteousness is the material cause of our salvation.

---

16. Westminster Divines, *Westminster Confession of Faith*.

17. This view seems to be endorsed by early Franciscans such as Alexander of Hales. See O'Collins and Rafferty, "Roman Catholic View," 279.

Westminster:

(P1) Infused righteousness is not part of our justificatory story.

(P2) Faith is the sole instrument for our justification.

Trent:

(C1) Infused righteousness is the sole formal cause of our justification.

(C2) Baptism is the sole instrument for our justification.

We have our first genuine contradictions. (P1) and (P2) are inconsistent with (C1) and (C2). Let IT stand for Imputation Theory and IF stand for Infusion theory. In what follows, I'd like to examine the biblical evidence for the doctrine of positive imputation. I'll argue that the doctrine is far from "clearly taught" in the New Testament. If IT and IF predict the texts discussed below equally well, the texts then are likely underdetermined. We first turn our attention to Romans 4:1–5:

> What then shall we say was gained by Abraham, our forefather according to the flesh? 2 For if Abraham was justified by works, he has something to boast about, but not before God. 3 For what does the Scripture say? "Abraham believed God, and it was counted to him as righteousness." 4 Now to the one who works, his wages are not counted as a gift but as his due. 5 And to the one who does not work but believes in him who justifies the ungodly, his faith is counted as righteousness...

Douglas Moo interprets Paul in 4:3 to suggest that Abraham lacks inherent righteousness since the analogy Abraham is involved in compares Abraham to the "ungodly."[18] The idea being that the righteousness must be purely be forensic since the "ungodly" clearly aren't inherently righteous. Therefore, Abraham must also lack inherent righteousness when he is declared righteous. The righteousness involved in Romans 4, then, is purely extrinsic in nature.

Of course, James Dunn doesn't think we should interpret the "ungodly" as morally bad individuals. Rather, "[t]hey are ungodly because they are outside the covenant. The good news here, is that "God justifies (that is, through the covenant) the ungodly (the one who is outside the covenant, that is, outside the sphere of God's saving righteousness)."[19]

---

18. Moo, *Epistle to the Romans*, 261–66.
19. Dunn, *Romans*, 205.

Many trees have been sacrificed in the last few decades over how best to interpret "believes" (*pistis*) in this passage. One approach is to argue that faith here is more plausibly rendered as embodied faith or faithfulness. Brant Pitre, Michael Barber, and John Kincaid make this case as they state the following:

> While Paul does employ *pistis* to signify belief in particular propositions as well as trust, he employs the term to signify true faithfulness or fidelity. In Galatians 3:23–26 Paul speaks about the coming of Christ and the revealing of faith almost interchangeably such that the person of Christ is not only the object of faith but also the revelation of what faithfulness constitutes. This broader meaning is also evident when Paul speaks of "the faithfulness of God" (Romans 3:3).[20]

I'm not sure if this debate is even necessary, however. Let's say that *pistis* should be rendered purely as propositional assent. And in the context of faith, we know that faith is a gift from God or a supernatural grace (Eph 2:8–9). What enables the subject to be declared as righteous is not the righteousness of Christ, at least that's not directly what is being discussed here. But rather, it is the subject's faith that reckons her righteous. There is no evidence for imputation here. One can deny that positive imputation occurs and still think that the subject gets to be declared righteous because of their propositional assent. Nonetheless, believing in God's promises, or more specifically, having faith, is a virtue. Virtues are not had by individuals who wholly lack righteousness. In this case, the subject is being declared righteous because there is some virtue the subject possesses. Of course, both the Catholic and the Protestant will want to say that God is ultimately the cause of faith. So, the question becomes how does God produce belief in the subject? Infusion perhaps? Let's move on.

1 Corinthians 1:30:

> And because of him you are in Christ Jesus, who became to us wisdom from God, righteousness and sanctification and redemption . . .

Doesn't this passage clearly teach imputation? We read straightforwardly that Christ is our righteousness. So, case closed, no? Not so fast. It simply does not follow that because Christ is our righteousness, that Westminster's doctrine of imputation must be true. To think that it follows misconstrues

---

20. Pitre, Barber, and Kincaid, *Paul, a New Covenant Jew*, 185.

PART I: THE GOSPEL

IF. Infusionists believe that sinners are made righteous only through the righteousness of Christ. Trent is clear on this position. Instead, what the infusionist says is that the righteousness of Christ becomes intrinsic to the sinner. That is, Christ righteousness is infused into the sinner. IF predicts Paul declaring that Christ is his righteousness just as well as the Westminster's imputation theory.

Moreover, if this passage was arguing for imputation of Christ righteousness, we'd expect this passage to also be teaching that wisdom and sanctification are also imputed to us. As N. T. Wright cleverly notes, "If 1 Corinthians 1:30 is forced to teach imputed righteousness, then we should then also have to speak, presumably of 'imputed wisdom,' 'imputed sanctification,' and 'imputed redemption,' a reading for which there is no support."[21] Let's now move on to what I take to be better candidates for passages teaching imputation.

> 2 Corinthians 5: 21: For our sake he made him to be sin who knew no sin, so that in him we might become the righteousness of God.

Once again, it isn't clear to me how this text is supposed to be evidence for IT, if IF advocates argue that their righteousness is not their own. The creaturely subject is only righteous when the subject receives Christ's righteousness. There isn't disagreement between IT and IF advocates with respect to obtaining the righteousness of God. The question is rather if one obtains it in a purely extrinsic sense or not. If anything, this passage could be read in favor of it.

N. T. Wright makes the case that it does:

> The little word *genōmetha* in 2 Corinthians 5:21b—"that we might become God's righteousness in him"—does not sit comfortably with the normal interpretation, according to which God's righteousness is "imputed" or "reckoned" to believers. If that was what Paul meant, with the overtones of "extraneous righteousness" that normally come with that theory, the one thing he ought not to have said is that we "become" that righteousness. Surely that leans far too much toward a Roman Catholic notion of infused righteousness.[22]

Moreover, as Pitre, Barber, and Kincaid point out,

---

21. Wright, *Justification*, 157.
22. Wright, *Justification*, 165.

"God made him to be sin" is best read as indicating that Jesus became an atoning sacrifice; in saying Christ was made to be "sin [hamarita]" (2 Corinthians 5:21), Paul is employing the language used in Israel's scriptures, where a "sin offering" can simply be sin [hamartia]" (Lev 4:33 LXX). In addition, though Christ does not become a sinner, Paul believes that Jesus actually bears the consequences of sin redemptively. Christ is not simply "considered" an atoning sacrifice, he actually offers himself as such a sacrifice. As a result, it is difficult to conclude that this verse teaches that the righteousness believers receive is merely juridical. If Christ actually bears the consequence of sin, then why insist believers do not actually become righteous?[23]

Finally, let's look at Philippians 3:8–9:

> Indeed, I count everything as loss because of the surpassing worth of knowing Christ Jesus my Lord. For his sake I have suffered the loss of all things and count them as rubbish, in order that I may gain Christ 9 and be found in him, not having a righteousness of my own that comes from the law, but that which comes through faith in Christ, the righteousness from God that depends on faith . . .

Here, we read that we have a righteousness from God by faith. Isn't this what you would expect on IT? I do take it that I find this passage to be the most persuasive out of all of the passages surveyed. Nonetheless, where does our faith come from? Even our faith is a gift from God (Eph 2:8–10). As discussed earlier, faith is a supernatural virtue. Since virtues are righteous features of a creature, we can conclude that the subject is more than merely forensically righteous. One intrinsically is already in possession of Christ's righteousness. This of course is due to their union with Christ. As E. P. Sanders puts it:

> Having righteousness by faith is the same as sharing the death and resurrection of Christ. The meaning of these conjoined formulations cannot be "a juridical decision that imputes righteousness to human beings although they are not in fact righteous." The meaning is born by the terminology of the mystical participation of the believer in Christ.[24]

Prothro takes Paul in Philippians 3:8–9 to be describing the process of how we are initially justified before God.

---

23. Pitre, Barber, and Kincaid, *Paul, a New Covenant Jew,* 182.
24. Sanders, *Paul,* 612–13.

PART I: THE GOSPEL

> Within the legal metaphor, this initial "justification" is the act of an accuser holding his opponent to be in the right, which involves forgiveness and effects reconciliation between them, and marks the beginning of a life of allegiance to God until the final day. But the means by which it occurs is the participatory transfer, and this transfer is transformative. Being made God's friend, freed from allegiance to sin, happens because one is joined to Christ's death and life through the Spirit. One "receives the gift of righteousness" (Rom 5:17) and "has righteousness" (Phil 3:9) in Christ, granted the status of an heir and its real rewards. But the foundation of this adoption—the very mechanism by which it occurs—is "the Spirit of [God's} Son" dwelling in them (Gal 4:5–7 cf. Rom 8:12–17).[25]

As Michael Gorman famously points out,[26] it is Galatians 2:15–20 that tells us how sinners become righteous. It is through co-crucifixion:

> [15] We ourselves are Jews by birth and not Gentile sinners; [16] yet we know that a person is not justified by works of the law but through faith in Jesus Christ, so we also have believed in Christ Jesus, in order to be justified by faith in Christ and not by works of the law, because by works of the law no one will be justified. [17] But if, in our endeavor to be justified in Christ, we too were found to be sinners, is Christ then a servant of sin? Certainly not! [18] For if I rebuild what I tore down, I prove myself to be a transgressor. [19] For through the law I died to the law, so that I might live to God. [20] I have been crucified with Christ. It is no longer I who live, but Christ who lives in me. And the life I now live in the flesh I live by faith in the Son of God, who loved me and gave himself for me.

I take it then, that IT isn't sufficiently well-motivated. There is no need to embrace IT as a doctrine. Moreover, Westminster Confession notwithstanding, the confessions surveyed do not even require IT. Nonetheless, Catholics and Protestants are in agreement. As Pope Benedict points out, *Sola Fide* is true. Nonetheless, as the Protestant Confessions make clear, it is never a faith that is alone. It is always accompanied by hope and charity. Moreover, while Scripture speaks an eschatological judgement based on works, both Catholics and Protestants agree that the only works that will stand the test of judgement are the merits of Christ himself. It is his righteousness that enable sinners to become declared just forevermore.

---

25. Prothro, *Pauline Theology of Justification*, 190.
26. Gorman, *Apostle of the Crucified Lord*.

All this to say we don't need to say that Catholics or Protestants believe in a different gospel. No. The kerygma, strictly speaking, is the same. Nor do we even need to conceive of Catholics and Protestants disagreeing on how the gospel makes right a sinner. There is logical space for the Protestant to agree with the Catholic. Ultimately, at the end of the day, it is Christ's righteousness that saves us. Having now laid out what the gospel is, who is called to share it, and how the gospel justifies the sinner, we move to the next section of the volume.

Part II

The Model

3

A Model from the Saints

In Michael Green's seminal work, *Evangelism in the Early Church*,[1] Green argues that the early church was successful in her evangelism, in part, by publicly displaying a counterculturual, revolutionary lifestyle. The church saw dignity in the poor and the abandoned. She raised infants left for dead. She lived in such a way that the first were last and the last were first. Individual members of the church built relationships with their neighbors and their neighbors took notice. The kerygma was shared and taken seriously, especially in the cities.

Of course, nothing furthered the gospel more than Christian martyrdom. Christianity was revolutionary, and to a pagan's ear, it could seem completely remarkable or not of this world. Once Christianity became legalized the full Christianization of the Roman Empire was all but inevitable. Nonetheless, evangelism took place after the Roman Empire was baptized. In this chapter, I want survey at models for evangelism that were implemented after the Edict of Milan. While there is no "one size fits all" evangelism method, it's plausible that significant saints and missionaries of the past provide important insights for us today. This chapter will survey important figures throughout Christendom who were known for their evangelism. At the end of the chapter, I plan to summarize the insights from this survey and develop a normative model for evangelism.

---

1. Green, *Evangelism in the Early Church*.

PART II: THE MODEL

Saint Patrick

Captured by Irish pirates in his youth, Patrick lived life as a slave in Ireland for over half a decade. Here, Patrick is introduced to the Irish culture, language, and belief system. Nonetheless, believing that God had called him to escape slavery, Patrick did just that—he escaped. After studying and becoming an ordained bishop, Patrick was eventually sent back to Ireland as a missionary to the people he once knew. Patrick of course becomes a very successful missionary and is responsible for baptizing thousands of Irish natives.

Given Patrick's success, it seems plausible that we could learn from his model of evangelism. Few people, after all, are credited with the conversion of a whole country. While details of his method are sparse, following Roy Flechner's work,[2] we do know his broad strategy. Preaching was a significant part of Patrick's mission. Nonetheless, Patrick seems to have implemented a top-down strategy.[3] Patrick would convert the mature children of tribe rulers and kings. Not only would he convert them, often they would enter into monastic life. This of course, created an environment that made thinking about monastic or clerical life possible for the average Irish subject.

Before baptizing the new believers, Patrick would catechize the newcomers, often during the Lenten season. He would teach them the basics of the faith, such as important doctrines that were to be believed, a basic ethical code, and how to pray.[4] Patrick's approach to evangelism as initiation fits well with what we have discussed in our first chapter.

Before you were baptized by Patrick, a slightly more expansive version of the Nicene Creed was required to be cited.[5] Patrick would then move on from city to city looking for more converts. Before leaving the baptized, however, Patrick would ordain clerics who would be left in charge. We are led to believe that Patrick ordained many to the priestly life and likely the diaconate.[6]

Driving much of Patrick's evangelism was his belief that he was ushering in the eschatological age to come. Before the imminent return of Christ, the gospel needed to go out to all nations. And from Patrick's

---

2. Flechner, *Saint Patrick Retold*.
3. Flechner, *Saint Patrick Retold*, 165.
4. Flechner, *Saint Patrick Retold*, 174–75.
5. Flechner, *Saint Patrick Retold*, 173.
6. Flechner, *Saint Patrick Retold*, 178.

perspective, Ireland was on the outer parts of the known world. Patrick, then, was properly motivated to keep his missionary activity going, even when persecution came.

Of course, it wasn't enough to preach the gospel and to catechize. Saint Patrick had to embody Christ. He had to become a little Christ to the Irish natives. While we can see Patrick's Christlikeness best through his confessions, I now turn to another evangelist who embodies Christ to the degree of even possessing the stigmata.

St. Francis

When one thinks of St. Francis it is hard to avoid thinking of Christ. Francis rid himself of his wealth and inheritance for a life dedicated to God. Francis is known for his poverty, his stewardship of creation, and his sacrificial love for his brothers and God. Francis embodied Christ in his evangelism and in his life.

The life of Christ was his model for evangelism. According to Adrian House, Francis once asked his brothers why he should continue to preach the gospel when he wasn't very good at it. Perhaps Francis thought it would be better to live a life of prayer. Francis apparently didn't have a high view of his preaching and the fruit it would produce. Nonetheless, Francis thought that he ought to leave his prayer time for preaching the gospel since we know Christ left his prayer time with the Father for the preaching of the gospel.[7] What followed Francis's preaching was reported miracle after miracle. Francis seemed to be a visible image of the unseen Christ.

Francis was extremely bold in his evangelistic approach. Francis did not try to hide his evangelistic concerns, even at times when it would behoove him to do so. At one point, Francis became a missionary during the Fifth Crusade. Francis grew tired of seeing the death of his colleagues and he decided he would try to get caught by the Muslims and then convert the sultan, Al-Kamil.

It is reported that Francis was up-front with the sultan that he wanted to the sultan to repent and be baptized. Francis would spend time with the sultan pleading for his conversion. It is reported that the sultan at one point replied that he could not convert because it would forfeit his life and throne.[8] Nonetheless, Francis lovingly pursued the sultan's conver-

---

7. Bonaventure, *Life of Saint Francis of Assisi*, 97–98.
8. House, *Francis of Assisi*, 213.

sion and he believed that, with God's grace, this was a real possibility. While ultimately the sultan remained Muslim, he released Francis and offered generous concessions to end the war. This points to there being mutual respect between the sultan and Francis. In a sense, then, Francis's encounter with the sultan acts as a model for religious discussion. We can make an attempt to change each other's mind about religion, and yet, at the end of the day, realize that we share much in common and wish for the well-being of the other.

One could summarize Francis's model for evangelism as follows: Whatever Christ did, do that. If Christ preached the gospel, we should preach the gospel. If Christ delivered the good news of the kingdom to the poor, we should too. Francis wanted to embody Christ in all things. In fact, Francis embodied Christ to the point where he possessed the stigmata. Of course, you as a twenty-first-century reader might be skeptical of such claims. Nonetheless, there is modest evidence to suggest that Francis did possess the stigmata. And if Francis possessed the stigmata, the stigmata could be seen as a vindication or endorsement of Francis's Christocentric evangelism model. Perhaps even those who are inclined to see their calling as to simply pray could be convinced that they too must step out on occasion and follow in the footsteps of Christ.

So what is the evidence? According to Bonaventure, many people were eyewitnesses to the stigmata. Bonaventure argues that among others, there were various cardinals who claimed to have seen the stigmata, Pope Alexander also claimed to be an eyewitness, and at the time of his death, over fifty brothers and St. Clare were witnesses to it.[9]

Three objections

The Bad Academic Argument:

> Maybe St. Bonaventure is a bad academic and is overly naive. Perhaps he came into contact with some "hearsay" and didn't check his sources. Or maybe Bonaventure is such a St. Francis supporter that he himself simply made up the accounts so that St. Francis would appear legendary.

Well, I doubt many people who thoroughly read Bonaventure will come away thinking that Bonaventure was a bad academic or scholar. His

---

9. Bonaventure, *Life of Saint Francis of Assisi*, 112.

brilliance rivals most of his medieval counterparts. He was a senior faculty member at the University of Paris and taught alongside St. Thomas. In some ways, his thought is similar to St. Thomas's (e.g., God is Pure Act and doesn't belong in any genus), but in other ways, he gives his own original account of knowledge of the divine and develops a wonderfully unique hermeneutical system for understanding nature's book. I think it would be our unjustified, modern-day biases that would lead us away in thinking that he must have just been terribly naive or willing to use false data for his academic agenda. I don't find this sort of reasoning persuasive.

The Lying Objection

The pope lied. The cardinals lied. St. Clare and the fifty brothers lied, and so on. Now, you might be tempted to think that the Catholic Church is corrupt and its members cannot be trusted. But, for those who don't think this way, it seems that until we are given reason to doubt their testimony, we have reason to accept it.

The Leprosy Objection

Perhaps the objector wants to argue that St. Francis had contracted leprosy and interpreted it as the stigmata. This is consistent with St. Bonaventure being a fine academic. The error occurs not in Bonaventure or his sources, but rather interpreting a medical condition. Now, you might think that there is some plausibility to this. St. Francis did meet and feed lepers. However, were the cardinals, pope, fifty brothers, St. Clare, and others totally ignorant to what leprosy looks like? I imagine not, since many of them would have ministered to those with leprosy. Moreover, surely the leprosy would have spread throughout Francis's body, making it obvious that there wasn't a stigmata but something de facto eating his flesh.

Perhaps we have good reason to think that the leprosy didn't spread or could be contained to the relevant parts of the body. Isn't all of this a little too serendipitous? If St. Francis in fact had leprosy in a religious context and the leprosy neatly painted a picture of the stigmata, it seems plausible to think there is still something miraculous here. The timing, setting, and containment of the leprosy would all happen to work in such a way as to make it seem like St. Francis had the stigmata. And in fact, it seems sufficiently miraculous that it could be said that God did give St.

Francis the stigmata and did so through natural processes. And if there is some reason to think that Francis had the stigmata, there is some reason to think his model of evangelism has been vindicated.

Jesuit Evangelism

We now move to discuss the practice of evangelism in the Far East, specifically, through one of the Church's greatest evangelists, Matteo Ricci. The Portuguese-born priest arrived in Macau in 1582. Ricci would learn Mandarin there and treat Macao as his base for future missions. There, men were trained to become pastors and evangelists for the Far East. Men like St. Andrew Kim Taegon, the great evangelist of Korea, were formed. Macau was the base for foreign missions in the Far East for the centuries.

Ricci's goal was to evangelize in the mainland China. Originally, Ricci thought his audience would be mostly Buddhists. In fact, he started his mission to China dressing in Buddhist attire. Ricci understood that the gospel would need to be enculturated. Quickly, however, Ricci found that his audience didn't mostly consist of Buddhists, but rather Confucians and Daoists. Ricci again dressed accordingly.

He did not approach the Chinese as if their views and way of living were all wrong. Ricci firmly believed that all truth was God's truth. He affirmed that God had a secret presence amongst the Chinese. Ricci sought to elevate Chinese customs and show how their ultimate meaning was discovered in Christ. R. Po-Chia Hsia puts Ricci evangelistic approach as follows:

> And leading the way to conversion, Ricci believed, would be the "Confucian scholars, who had always governed China . . . and [who] never speak of supernatural things, and are almost completely in agreement with us in ethics."[10] By not disputing the Confucian scholars, but in interpreting their teachings in the manner of Christianity, and in suggesting this was indeed the way of their own ancient sages, "many of them have become Christians and give manifest signs of being good Christians, going to confession and receiving communion, and showing themselves, to their own strength and will, their love of our holy faith."[11]

---

10. Hsia, *Jesuit in the Forbidden City*.
11. Hsia, *Jesuit in the Forbidden City*, 283.

Ricci would go on to write *The True Meaning of the Lord of Heaven*.[12] The volume acted as a tract to get educated Chinese to take seriously the claims of Christianity. In the form of a discussion between a Christian and an educated Chinese man, Ricci argues that the Chinese originally believed in God but that the introduction to the foreign philosophy of Buddhism made the Chinese forget who they worshipped. Ricci spends the first part of the book explicating Chinese philosophy and then moves to argue for God's existence. Ricci argues for God's existence via standard Thomistic proofs. The overall point of the volume is to argue that the Lord of Heaven found in Chinese literature is actually Jesus. Ricci moves on to answer objections to God's existence, such as "who caused God?" This eventually leads Ricci to refute Daoist and Buddhist philosophies. Ricci knew that if he was going to reach the Chinese, he had to know what the Chinese believed, at times even better than the Chinese themselves.

Learning Chinese language, customs, culture, and religious philosophy was more important to Ricci than most things. Ricci thought the key to getting genuine converts who would become zealous for the faith, was to truly understand his field. Hsia puts it like this:

> Summing up a lifetime's experience in China, Ricci thought it better to have a small, high quality Christian community than a large multitude. Specifically, it was far more important for the Jesuits to know Chinese well than to have another 10,000 new baptisms: "to know our own without knowing theirs serves nothing . . . I myself value it [knowledge of Chinese letters] more than another ten thousand converts, since this is the way of for the universal conversion of the realm."[13]

When all was said and done, Ricci spent twelve years in Guangdong and helped baptize around 120 Chinese. Ricci eventually moved into the country's capital. In his first two years, he helped baptize seventy individuals.[14] Many who were baptized were scholars and political influencers in their own right. Ricci went after zealous Daoists and Confucians and turned them into zealous Christians. Ricci did not manipulate the weak or uniformed. Ricci instead had a different idea. Ricci went after the educated, the affluent, and those who had political capital. If Ricci could get hold of

---

12. For more on the following summary of *True Meaning of the Lord of Heaven*, see Hsia, *Jesuit in the Forbidden City*, 224–44.

13. Hsia, *Jesuit in the Forbidden City*, 282.

14. Hsia, *Jesuit in the Forbidden City*, 246.

PART II: THE MODEL

those who had power and influence, he could eventually reach the masses. Ultimately, Ricci had the emperor on his mind. Sadly, he would never end up meeting the emperor, though from a distance Ricci received his favor.

Revivalism in America: The First Great Awakening

From 1740–1743 revival broke out in New England, the effects of which would trickle down to the South over the next couple of decades. The Great Awakening solidified both the future of Christianity in America as well as give it its Evangelical flair. There was unmistakable message that America sent to the world through these revivals. Anyone, at any time, could encounter Christ's Spirit. It didn't matter how educated one was, or whether one was a clergy member or a lay person. Christ was very much alive, and he was waiting to be encountered.

Scholars typically trace the origins of the Great Awakening to the Reformation. One needn't be a priest or a mystic to get to Christ. Christ is personal and can be known by whoever seeks him. As Thomas Kidd puts it, "Most historians, however, trace Evangelicalism's origins to sources within the European churches of the Protestant Reformation, which began in the early sixteenth century. A number of reformers with Protestantism criticized their own church for teaching a formal, cold religion instead of a vital, personal relationship with God."[15] Much of European religion faced a similar problem: dead religion. One could affirm the creeds and attend weekly services, but lack a robust and personal relationship with Christ. The First and Second Great Awakening attempted to correct this.

While the space in this volume is limited, I'd like to highlight the main character from the First Great Awakening in hopes of helping us develop an evangelistic methodology. While, explicating its greatest public defender, Jonathan Edwards, would be interesting, but I have chosen to discuss its greatest evangelist, George Whitefield.

Before becoming an evangelist, Whitefield was an actor. As you might have guessed, Whitefield would use his acting talents to help deliver his sermons. These sermons were not monotone monologues. No. Whitefield acted through his sermons, captivating his audience by the thousands. His

---

15. Kidd, *Great Awakening*, 3.

primary goal of evangelism was to get the masses to accept Christ's sacrificial life for the forgiveness of their sins.[16]

Whitefield often got in trouble for how ecumenical he was. Whitefield ministered with Congregationalists, Baptists, Presbyterians, and of course, those within his own tradition, Anglicanism. While he had his disagreements with the Wesley brothers over the so-called doctrines of grace, he had great admiration for them as well.

Perhaps the great contribution that Whitefield brought was reviving the old practice of open-air preaching. Whitefield didn't purely preach in parishes. His primary method of evangelism was to preach in the streets, in fields, and anywhere else where people could gather and listen. Whitefield brought Christianity to the unchurched.

Revivalism in America: The Second Great Awakening

Now, I could of course discuss how evangelism played out in the nineteenth century during the Second Great Awakening by way of discussing the likes of D. L. Moody or Charles Finney. Instead, I'd like to look at Catholic revivalism that occurred toward the end of the Second Great Awakening.

In *Catholic Revivalism*,[17] James Dolan shows that in the early 1800s the Catholic Church as a mission was in pretty terrible shape. He notes, for example, that there were places in the country where for every 1 priest there were about 5,555 laypersons.[18] A lot of cities lacked a full-time priest and even a church building. Depending on the area, the best situation one could hope for was a designated log cabin where mass would be held occasionally. Fast-forward to 1908, and the Church in America is thriving in more ways than one and it is no longer labeled as a mission.[19] What happened?

Since Catholics were so spread out and there weren't enough priests, chapels started to host "missions" (i.e., revivals). Some of them would last for a week or two. The priest would catechize through his sermons throughout the day and by night preach dramatic and endearing sermons, often revolving around salvation. As first and second waves of Irish and Eastern European immigration hit America, many (perhaps most)

16. Kidd, *Great Awakening*, 43.
17. Dolan, *Catholic Revivalism*.
18. Dolan, *Catholic Revivalism*, 8.
19. Dolan, *Catholic Revivalism*, 1.

nonpracticing Catholics arrived. These missions would then take newly immigrated Catholics and catch them up to speed on the kerygma and sacramental theology.[20]

By the 1850s, missions were the primary method of evangelization for the Church in the States. There were even priests who for twenty or thirty years, as their primary vocation, preached across the country for the missions. In contrast with some of the more well-known Protestants in the Second Great Awakening, these priests were often very educated and oftentimes the author of various papers and scholarly books (e.g., Clarence Walworth). Eventually, the Church became strong enough to try to minister to non-Catholic Christians as well. By the early 1900s, the Church was both prosperous and influential. Finally, we have a recognizable Catholic institution in America.

Billy Graham and Pope John Paul II

In some sense, I have told a brief story about how American Protestantism and Catholicism developed. Before I develop a model for evangelism that is informed by the historical methods surveyed, I'd like to briefly discuss two twentieth-century evangelists, each one a representative of the aforementioned traditions.

In 1972, John Paul II started an evangelistic movement in the Catholic Church. John Paul II called the Church to participate in what he called the New Evangelization. The idea is simple: The old world evangelized the Americas five hundred years ago. Now, as Christianity has lost its hold on Europe, it is time for the Americas to evangelize Europe.[21]

In his later encyclical *Redemptoris Missio*, John Paul II makes it clear that the Church is far from completing its mission to evangelize the world. Rather, he argued that we needed to take seriously our call to evangelize and see that mission as "urgent." John Paul II makes it clear that Jesus is in fact the only way to God. And while God can save those who aren't explicitly Catholic and give them a mysterious relationship to the Church (see 1:10), we have a duty to evangelize all persons. Even those who can be saved in a mysterious way by Christ need, for their own well-being and the well-being of the common good, to have a formal and explicit relationship with the Church. The

---

20. Dolan, *Catholic Revivalism*, 26–42.
21. Hahn, *Evangelizing Catholics*, 22.

message that we should preach is the kerygma, that is, the death, burial, and resurrection of Christ for the forgiveness of sin (2:16).

John Paul II traveled the world preaching this message to some of the largest crowds the world has ever seen. He even preached this message in dangerous places like Poland during its communist era. In fact, he is widely credited with playing an important role in the Soviet Union's collapse. Knowing that non-Catholics needed to be initiated into Catholic life, John Paul II promulgated the first modern-day universal catechism of the Catholic Church.

Visually however, it was John Paul II's calling for World Youth Days that encapsulates the evangelical aspects of his papacy. Every four years, the Church, especially its young people, gather in a specific city. Bishops, priests, and lay scholars, along with the Pope, meet together to give kerygma-centered talks to residents of the relevant city and to the Church at large. In some ways, what John Paul II did was replicate what we see in America's revivalism period. World Youth Day follows the Protestant Great Awakening method of sending preachers to give talks in fields and to preach in the open air of a city.

Of course, in the Protestant world, there is no greater preacher from the twentieth century than Billy Graham. Graham is known for utilizing the method of "crusades" to preach the gospel. Similar to how Catholic parishes would advertise for special revival meetings in the nineteenth century, Graham would advertise for a crusade in a large church building, and even at times, a stadium. People from all over the city would come to hear this simple man preach about God saving sinners through his Son, Jesus Christ. Graham's message of forgiveness and love was the same message that his revivalist counterparts in the First and Second Great Awakenings preached. God sent his Son to die for humanity's sins on the cross. By "accepting Christ's sacrifice," we too can have our sins forgiven and be members of God's kingdom.

Like Whitefield, Graham was known for being ecumenical. He allied with Catholics and Protestants of every kind to announce the gospel. Graham saw evangelism as primarily a way to initiate nonbelievers into Christianity. Since Catholics and mainstream Protestants share the same gospel, Catholics and Protestants could support one another in attracting conversions. In fact, Graham's cooperation with Catholics led to the formation of Catholic and Evangelical alliances when it came to the future culture wars.

PART II: THE MODEL

A Normative Model for Evangelism

While there is no "one" model for evangelism, I think we can derive plausible insights from the aforementioned saints. We can call this model The Saints Model (TSM). Patrick, Francis, and a likely future saint, Ricci, took a top-down approach to evangelism. Patrick looked to convert the princes and princesses of the local Irish kingdoms. Ricci looked to convert the political affluent and those well-versed in Confucianism. And Francis looked to end a holy war by going straight for the sultan's conversion. Similarly, it seems plausible that the church should look for figures in society who have symbolic capital. She should seek to convert those who have real power in society. Of course, this shouldn't come at the sacrifice of the powerless. The church should continue to live in countercultural revolutionary ways. As the culture of death continues to thrive in the West, a church that once again comes to the aid of the powerless and defenseless speaks volumes. The church ought to embody Christ as Francis embodied Christ.

Nonetheless, living like Christ is not sufficient for evangelization. Evangelism requires preaching the kerygma. Like the revivalists before us, we ought to be intentional about sharing the kerygma. Following the success from the Catholic revivals of the nineteenth century, we should host special bishops and priests to preach the faith for an allotted period. We should continue making much of events that occur on a non-annual basis like World Youth Day, in hopes of building momentum and attract those from other faiths (or no faith at all). We should also be prepared to open our hands to Christians from other traditions to help deliver the good news. Nonetheless, what is clear from the lives of Saint Patrick and Ricci, we should take the time to understand the culture we are evangelizing too.

Finally, following John Paul II's lead, the church should never cease from its preaching that Jesus is the way, the truth, and the life. Jesus is the only way to God. Nonetheless, we should understand that God has ways that are not our ways. God has a secret presence in other religious contexts. Still, we have an obligation to preach Christ crucified to all. We should encounter other religious traditions as did Ricci and the Jesuits in the Far East. We should look for what is true and beautiful in the relevant tradition and show how their customs are elevated by the gospel. And ultimately, regardless if conversion happens, when we depart from our friends who do not share our faith, we leave with mutual respect and love for each other's well-being, as Francis did with the sultan. Having now presented a model for evangelism, I move to further discuss how a theology of other religions should inform TSM.

4

An Analytic Christology of Religions

In the Introduction, I informed the reader that while this book is intended to be a theology of evangelism for all Nicene Christians traditions, I am indeed ultimately a Catholic and will at times pull from the rich resources of the Catholic tradition.[1] This remains true. In this chapter, informed by Vatican II and one of its premier modern-day scholars, Gerald O'Collins, I will argue (1), that while the Christian evangelist should proclaim that Jesus is the only way to God, she should nonetheless be open to the possibility that Christ is saving those in non-Christian traditions as non-explicit or anonymous Christians, and, (2), that other serious religious traditions can be interpreted as doctrinally consistent with (or something nearby) the Nicene Christian tradition.

These theses will lead me to conclude that in the Christian's approach to evangelism, her first step in persuading her non-Christian counterpart, should be to emphasize commonality that exists between the Christian tradition and the relevant non-Christian tradition. The evangelist, then, shouldn't see her main task as developing arguments against her interlocutor's religious tradition (though theoretically, this has its place), but rather her focus should be on proclaiming an additional truth that her interlocutor can accept alongside many of her already held religious commitments. The strategy here is reminiscent of the Jesuit strategy discussed in chapter 3. In doing this, we will have further developed the TSM.

---

1. What follows is a revised paper that was published with Michael DeVito in *Religions*, "Christology of Religions and a Theology of Evangelism."

PART II: THE MODEL

O'Collins's Theology of Religions

In *A Christology of Religions*, Gerald O'Collins looks to develop a Christocentric theology for how Christians should understand non-Christian religious traditions. O'Collins first looks at New Testament passages where Jesus seems to be concerned with not only "God's people" but also the gentiles. The first passage O'Collins discusses is Mark 7:24–30. Jesus encounters a Syro-Phoenician woman (Matthew calls her a Canaanite in Matthew 15:21–28). The woman pleads for help on behalf of her demon-possessed daughter. While at first Jesus seemed to state that gentiles were dogs in some way, Jesus ends up declaring to the woman that "great is your faith." As O'Collins puts it, "A Gentile dared to ask him for a miracle, and he was willing to perform it—thus, he began breaking down the barriers that separated Jews and Gentiles. Even though she did not share in the special blessings of Jewish covenant with God and seemingly had enjoyed no previous contact with him, Jesus, according to Matthew, praised her 'great faith.'"[2]

O'Collins moves on to discuss the faith of a gentile centurion in Matthew 8:5–13. The centurion believed that a simple statement from Jesus would heal his son. Jesus' response was to say that "in no one in Israel have I found such faith."[3] Once again, O'Collins highlights how the faith of a gentile outsider was far greater than those, "who enjoyed the special revelation of God given through Abraham, Moses, the prophets, and various wisdom figures."[4] In Luke's version of this story, we also see Jesus state, "I tell you, many will come from the east and from the west and will eat with Abraham, Isaac, and Jacob in the kingdom of heaven, while the heirs of the kingdom will be thrown into outer darkness."

One other relevant passage worth mentioning is John 10:16, where Jesus states, "I have other sheep that do not belong to this fold. I must bring them also, and they will listen to my voice. So, there will be one flock, one shepherd." It's not uncommon for contemporary theologians to understand that the lost sheep that do not belong to "this fold" are gentiles who don't explicitly follow the God of Israel. Nonetheless, as O'Collins points out, Jesus stated that those who belong to his family (in this case "fold") are "Whoever does the will of God." As O'Collins states, "He did not specify as candidates for his new family 'all those Jews who do the will of God.'" Any

---

2. O'Collins, *Christology of Religions*, 4.
3. Unless specified, translations are from the NRSV.
4. O'Collins, *Christology of Religions*, 5.

man or woman—read now Buddhist, Confucian, follower of a traditional religion, Hindu, Muslim, Sikh, agnostic, and so forth—who does what God wants qualifies for admission to this new community and becomes, whether he or she knows it or not, truly related to Jesus, a "family member in the kingdom of God."[5]

In summary, Jesus praises the faith of gentiles in the highest terms available, again, those gentiles who were unlikely orthodox followers of the God of Israel. Jesus informs us that he has sheep that are not of the Jewish fold. These are gentiles who have no explicit awareness of the person of Jesus yet will "listen" to Jesus as the folds become one. In fact, given that Jesus informs us that it is "whoever does the will of God" belongs to his family, it's plausible to assume that these sheep that belong to him are, indeed, gentiles who implicitly follow the Father's will.

O'Collins moves from discussing Jesus' theology of religions to how theologians understand Jesus' priestly sacrifice.[6] There is a universal dimension in Christ's atonement. In fact, O'Collins references Cardinal John Henry Newman's work on the conscience to express how Jesus' triple office of priest, prophet, and king is manifested in the human conscience. Newman states, "Conscience is the aboriginal Vicar of Christ, a prophet in its information, a monarch in its peremptoriness, a priest in its blessings and anathemas, and, even though the eternal priesthood throughout the Church could cease to be, in it the sacerdotal principle would remain and would have sway."[7] O'Collins helpfully characterizes Newman's point by stating, "Here Newman presented the triple office as if it were a spiritual genetic code that preexisted any institutional structures and highlighted in particular 'the sacerdotal principle' as intrinsically shaping the human spirit."[8] As O'Collins shows, this fits well with Karl Rahner's theory of the sacerdotal existential. The sacerdotal existential is a kind of grace that primes a subject to accept the message of Christ. The rough idea is that Christian revelation already exists implicitly in the human person. We are in a sense designed for Christian revelation and are already inclined to accept it. Drawing from both Newman and Rahner, O'Collins states, "Through the sacerdotal existential, which is their conscience, human beings are positively preconditioned from within to share through baptism in the priesthood of

---

5. O'Collins, *Christology of Religions*, 10.
6. O'Collins, *Christology of Religions*, 51.
7. Newman, *On Priesthood of Christ*, 69–70.
8. O'Collins, *Christology of Religions*, 51.

Christ (and in his office as prophet and king). But they already experience that priesthood in the depths of their being and through the voice of their conscience."[9] In this way, humanity is already connected with Jesus, the ultimate high priest, who makes atonement for all. As O'Collins states, "The sacerdotal existential suggests the way in which Christ's priestly work has already shaped them before they ever have a chance of responding to what that work brings them in the offer of God's grace."[10] Christ's priestly work, then, enables those who are not of the Jewish fold to follow Jesus. They implicitly follow Jesus by following their conscience, which is connected to and shaped by the priestly work of Christ.

Vatican II and World Religions

In what follows, I will move my discussion from a theology of religions to specifically discussing the theology of religions at Vatican II. For my Protestant readers, I hope you can bear with me!

In *Nostra Aetate* (*NA*), we read the following:

> From ancient times down to the present, there is found among various peoples a certain perception of that hidden power which hovers over the course of things and over the events of human history; at times some indeed have come to the recognition of a Supreme Being, or even of a Father. This perception and recognition penetrates their lives with a profound religious sense. Religions, however, that are bound up with an advanced culture have struggled to answer the same questions by means of more refined concepts and a more developed language. Thus in Hinduism, men contemplate the divine mystery and express it through an inexhaustible abundance of myths and through searching philosophical inquiry. They seek freedom from the anguish of our human condition either through ascetical practices or profound meditation or a flight to God with love and trust. Again, Buddhism, in its various forms, realizes the radical insufficiency of this changeable world; it teaches a way by which men, in a devout and confident spirit, may be able either to acquire the state of perfect liberation, or attain, by their own efforts or through higher help, supreme illumination. Likewise, other religions found everywhere try to counter the restlessness of the human

---

9. O'Collins, *Christology of Religions*, 52.
10. O'Collins, *Christology of Religions*, 52.

heart, each in its own manner, by proposing "ways," comprising teachings, rules of life, and sacred rites. The Catholic Church rejects nothing that is true and holy in these religions. She regards with sincere reverence those ways of conduct and of life, those precepts and teachings which, though differing in many aspects from the ones she holds and sets forth, nonetheless often reflect a ray of that Truth which enlightens all men. Indeed, she proclaims, and ever must proclaim Christ "the way, the truth, and the life" (John 14:6), in whom men may find the fullness of religious life, in whom God has reconciled all things to Himself.[11]

There are a couple of things that I want to emphasize from this text. First, NA seems to affirm that from ancient times, people from all sorts of backgrounds and cultures have become aware of Divinity, or perhaps to put it slightly differently, the Other. That is, non-Jewish and non-Christian worshippers are still aware of Divinity's reality; that is the same Divinity that exists in the Jewish and Christian traditions. We are all in touch with the same reality.

Second, we should not only consider that practitioners of other religious traditions, like Buddhism and Hinduism, are aware of Divinity, we should also recognize that the Church "rejects nothing that is true and holy in these religions." Christians may rightly rejoice and commend the truth espoused in other religious traditions. One might even dare to kiss a holy book that contains many religious truths. After all, these truths are "holy."

Third, while other religious traditions have truth, the Church should never fail to preach Jesus as the only way to God. Now, one could make the following suggestion:

Jesus is truth incarnate. If these religious traditions are full of truth, then shouldn't we say that these religious traditions have Christ to some extent? Let's move on to *Lumen Gentium* 16 before we address this point:

LG 16

Finally, those who have not yet received the Gospel are related in various ways to the people of God. In the first place we must recall the people to whom the testament and the promises were given and from whom Christ was born according to the flesh. On account of their fathers this people remains most dear to God, for God does not repent of the gifts He makes nor of the calls He issues. But the plan of salvation also includes those who acknowledge the

---

11. *Nostra Aetate*, https://www.vatican.va/archive/hist_councils/ii_vatican_council/documents/vat-ii_decl_19651028_nostra-aetate_en.html.

Creator. In the first place amongst these there are the Muslims, who, professing to hold the faith of Abraham, along with us adore the one and merciful God, who on the last day will judge mankind. Nor is God far distant from those who in shadows and images seek the unknown God, for it is He who gives to all men life and breath and all things, and as Saviour wills that all men be saved. *Those also can attain to salvation who through no fault of their own do not know the Gospel of Christ or His Church, yet sincerely seek God and moved by grace strive by their deeds to do His will as it is known to them through the dictates of conscience. Nor does Divine Providence deny the helps necessary for salvation to those who, without blame on their part, have not yet arrived at an explicit knowledge of God and with His grace strive to live a good life. Whatever good or truth is found amongst them is looked upon by the Church as a preparation for the Gospel* [italicizing is my own doing]. She knows that it is given by Him who enlightens all men so that they may finally have life. But often men, deceived by the Evil One, have become vain in their reasonings and have exchanged the truth of God for a lie, serving the creature rather than the Creator. Or some there are who, living and dying in this world without God, are exposed to final despair. Wherefore to promote the glory of God and procure the salvation of all of these, and mindful of the command of the Lord, "Preach the Gospel to every creature," the Church fosters the missions with care and attention.[12]

In *LG* 16, we first see that Jews and Muslims "adore the one merciful God." While *NA* seems to support the view that non-Jews and non-Christians are aware of Divinity, we see this more explicitly stated with a specific reference to Islam. Moreover, it goes beyond *NA* in saying that we all "adore" this God. Muslims are seen as indeed loving the God of the Bible.

Second, we see a powerful statement regarding all those who do not explicitly confess faith in Christ. Looking at the italicized words, we see that those who, through no fault of their own, lack knowledge of the gospel and Christ's Church, yet moved by God's grace, follow God's will as it is known by the "dictates of conscience," and can still be saved. We read, "Whatever good or truth is found amongst them is looked upon by the Church as a preparation for the Gospel." God uses faith in what points to the gospel as if the faith was explicitly in the gospel. *Ad Gentes* (*AG*) can help us understand this more:

---

12. *Lumen Gentium*, https://www.vatican.va/archive/hist_councils/ii_vatican_council/documents/vat-ii_const_19641121_lumen-gentium_en.html.

> But whatever truth and grace are to be found among the nations, as a sort of secret presence of God, He frees from all taint of evil and restores to Christ its maker, who overthrows the devil's domain and wards off the manifold malice of vice. And so, whatever good is found to be sown in the hearts and minds of men, or in the rites and cultures peculiar to various peoples, not only is not lost, but is healed, uplifted, and perfected for the glory of God, the shame of the demon, and the bliss of men. Thus, missionary activity tends toward eschatological fullness. For by it the people of God is increased to that measure and time which the Father has fixed in His power(cf. Acts 1:7). To this people it was said in prophecy: "Enlarge the space for your tent, and spread out your tent cloths unsparingly" (Is. 54:2). By missionary activity, the mystical body grows to the mature measure of the fullness of Christ (cf. Eph. 4:13); and the spiritual temple, where God is adored in spirit and in truth (cf. John 4:23), grows and is built up upon the foundation of the Apostles and prophets, Christ Jesus Himself being the supreme corner stone (Eph. 2:20).[13]

We are told that truth and grace are found among the nations and that this enables God to have a "secret presence." Nonetheless, by proclaiming the gospel, those who had access to God are now maturing and are experiencing the "fullness of Christ." In this way, the rites and customs of cultures that are good are not thrown away but find their ultimate fulfillment in Christ. In fact, by saying that "truth and grace" are found in the nations, we see that in some sense, Christ is already in the nations and is at work, before the gospel is ever explicitly preached. As O'Collins notes, *AG* "picks up the Johannine terminology of 'truth and grace' (John 1:14, 17) to recognize how Christ, 'the author' of these elements, is already present among 'the nations' even before they hear the word of Christian preaching. As giver of gifts of revelation ('truth') and salvation ('grace'), he has already come to the nonevangelized, albeit mysteriously." Nonetheless, we are told in *AG* that we need to keep proclaiming the gospel so that cultures and the nations can "participate fully in the mystery of Christ." So, while it is true that those who from no fault of their own lack explicit knowledge that the gospel message is true, can indeed be saved, they are still saved by their implicit faith in Christ. And we should of course still be motivated to preach the gospel, so that those who are saved by implicit faith in Christ can participate fully in him.

13. *Ad Gentes*, https://www.vatican.va/archive/hist_councils/ii_vatican_council/documents/vat-ii_decree_19651207_ad-gentes_en.html.

PART II: THE MODEL

Having sketched a theology of religions in Vatican II, I now move briefly to discuss how the Roman Catholic view developed. Those familiar with the Church's tradition are likely familiar with the saying that "there is no salvation outside of the Church." As Francis Sullivan points out, there was a time when it was common to believe that the gospel had gone out to all people groups. To support this claim, Sullivan offers up Gregory of Nyssa when he states that, "But if in fact the call has gone out to all, with no difference on the account of rank, age or nation . . . how could it be right to blame God for the fact that his word has not achieved dominion over all?"[14] Sullivan also quotes Ambrose for evidence. Ambrose states, "For the Mercy of the Lord has been spread by the Church to all nations; the faith has been spread to all people."[15] Finally, Sullivan references Chrysostom's quote that "One should not think that ignorance excuses the non-believer . . . When you are ignorant of what can easily be known, you have to suffer the penalty."[16] Chrysostom seems to think that unbelievers can easily know the gospel, at least if they put in the effort. Because the gospel can be easily known to nonbelievers, they are indeed liable to judgment.

However, new reflections on the doctrine occurred when the New World was discovered. There were continents of people who never had access to the gospel. When theologian Domingo Soto reflected on the situation, he advocated that the people of the New World could be saved in the same way as those in the Old Testament were saved.[17] Around the same time, Albert Pigge developed the idea that some Muslims could be saved by possessing an implicit faith in Christ.[18] Of course, these themes will continue to develop as the Church comes to understand more and more how individuals may not culpably possess knowledge of the gospel. This makes plausible the claim that Vatican II's doctrine isn't so much an innovation brought about by twentieth-century liberalism, but rather is a doctrine that organically develops over time given reflection in various diverse contexts.

---

14. Sullivan, *Salvation Outside the Church?*, 25; Gregory of Nyssa, *Oratio catechetica* 30.

15. Sullivan, *Salvation Outside the Church?*, 25–26; Ambrose, 118 Sermo 8:57.

16. Sullivan, *Salvation Outside the Church?*; 26; John Chrysostom, *Epistle Ad Rom*, Hom. 26.3–4.

17. Sullivan, *Salvation Outside the Church?*, 20, 76; Domingo Soto, *De natura et gratia* (1547).

18. Sullivan, *Salvation Outside the Church?*, 81; Albert Pigge, *De libero hominis arbitrio*.

Having stated all this, I have made my case for the first part of my thesis for this chapter. I now move on to (2).

World Religions

While one could write a whole book (or maybe a few?) on how and to what extent various world religions can be seen as consistent with one another, for the purposes of this chapter, I simply want to sketch various approaches one could take to argue that serious religious traditions can be interpreted as doctrinally consistent with (or something nearby) the Nicene Christian tradition. In order to do this succinctly, I will not be able to explain the fundamentals of each religious tradition.[19] What I will do instead is assume that my reader has background knowledge of the religious traditions being discussed and I will simply offer up alternative or unique ways to understand how these religious traditions can be seen as consistent with Christianity. This means I will only bring up those doctrines which I see as most relevant for my task. This shouldn't by any means be seen as an exhaustive argument for a genuine synthesis but simply a way to show that the thesis is plausible. One final note before our exploration begins: I will not attempt to show how Christian belief is consistent with Judaism. This is because this book is assuming that the Christian message is true. And of course, in Christianity, the message and theology of the Messiah are supposed to be seen as consistent with the Tanakh.

Islam

Quranism is an Islamic school of thought that rejects that the *tafsir* and Hadith should be taken seriously or possess any important authority within the Islamic community. For a proponent of Quranism, the Qur'an is all that matters. The Hadith, it is argued, are not reliable and came about far later than the Qur'an, and often they came about in politically charged contexts. For the sake of this chapter, I will interpret Islam from these religious lenses. Of course, it must be acknowledged that those who endorse Quranism are by far in the minority. It does not matter. As stated, our interests are purely related to whether there is logical space to interpret Islam in such a way

---

19. For a survey on what world religions teach, see Baldwin and McNabb, *Plantingian Religious Epistemology and World Religions*.

PART II: THE MODEL

that it is consistent with Christian belief. Now, even by putting the Hadith and the *tafsir* aside, there are four main areas of potential conflict between Christianity and Islam that we will discuss in this section:

1. Jesus is God and the only begotten Son of God.
2. The Qur'an's denial of the doctrine of the Trinity.
3. Jesus died on the cross.
4. Muhammad is a prophet from God.

Abdulla Galadari has argued that the Qur'an can be read consistently with the Gospel of John.[20] This should come across as a surprise as the Gospel of John is the Gospel where Jesus is most explicitly called God and named the only begotten Son of God. Traditionally, Islamic theology denies these propositions. Having stated this, I will use Galadari's work to help resolve the tension behind (1). Galadari starts off his work by reminding his readers that at times the Qur'an suggests that Christians should use the Gospels to judge the revelation of the Qur'an:

> And let the People of the Gospel judge by what Allah has revealed therein. And whoever does not judge by what Allah has revealed—then it is those who are the defiantly disobedient. (Surah 5:47)[21]

One traditional interpretation to this text is to endorse the doctrine of abrogation. Roughly, the idea is that the later Surahs should trump or abrogate the earlier Surahs if there is theological conflict between the earlier and later passages. In this case, passages that will later explicitly deny that Jesus is begotten or passages that seem to assume that Jesus is not God, will change our understanding of passages like Surah 5:47, which seems to indicate that the Gospels are consistent with the Qur'an. One such passage that is used to demonstrate that Jesus is not God is Surah 9:30–31:

> The Jews say: "Ezra ('Uzayr) is Allah's son [Ibn]," and the Christians say: "The Messiah is the son [Ibn] of Allah." These are merely verbal assertions in imitation of the sayings of those unbelievers who preceded them.[30] May Allah ruin them. How do they turn away from the Truth? They take their rabbis and their monks for their lords apart from Allah, and also the Messiah, son of Mary, whereas they were commanded to worship none but the One True

---

20. Galadari, *Qur'anic Hermeneutics*.
21. Sahih International translation unless otherwise noted.

God. There is no god but He. Exalted be He above those whom they associate with Him in His Divinity.

On the surface of this passage, it seems that the Messiah (Jesus) is not the Son (Ibn) of God. Apparently, stating that "the Messiah is not the Son of God" is something unbelievers do. We are then told that "they take their rabbis and their monks for their lords apart from Allah, and also the Messiah Son of Mary . . ." This passage is a bit puzzling for several reasons. First off, Jews don't believe that Ezra is the son of God. So, it isn't obvious that we should interpret Ibn as a literal son. Instead, assuming that Muhammad knew what he was talking about, Galardari, looking at how the book of Ezra uses the Hebrew word 'bn' (to build), suggests we interpret Ibn here to mean house. This way, the passage is condemning the relevant persons who claim Ezra as the temple of God (Ezra of course being the person who is primarily responsible for the Second Temple's existence) and Jesus as the temple of God. But are they being condemned for their beliefs? Galardari suggests that they are not but rather are being condemned for being hypocritical:

> This suggests that the Messiah should not be God but that they should worship God alone. In these Qur'anic passages, it seems that when the Qur'an uses the term "with their mouths (*bi-afwāhihim*)" it is contrasted that what they say with their mouths is not the same as it is in their hearts. Also, Qur'an 9:30 mentions that when the Jews and Christians say things with their mouths, they imitate the unbelievers of before using the term "*kafarū*." This term is also found in Qur'an 3:167 and 5:41, as mentioned above. This could make use of a different understanding of the Qur'anic passage. If the Jews and Christians are making a claim about the Temple of God, it is nothing but a saying with their mouths, implying it is not in their hearts.[22]

In personal correspondence, Galardari tells me that in Arabic, the Surah can read differently:

> In the Arabic text, it says they have taken their rabbis and monks as lords instead of God and the Messiah . . . The way it is recited makes it as if grammatically the Messiah though mentioned after God to be conjoined with the rabbis and monks based on the ending vowel. Arabic of course was not written with vowels in its earliest literary form including the Qur'an. Due to the peculiarity of this text, there is equal if not even possibly higher probability

22. Galadari, *Qur'anic Hermeneutics*, 90.

PART II: THE MODEL

> that the Messiah is conjoined with God and not with the rabbis and monks.[23]

If Galadari is right, then there is no reason to think that this text is at odds with the Gospel of John. In fact, if anything, the "Messiah" being conjoined with the word "God" would be evidence for the deity of the Messiah.

Let's say that Galadari is wrong in his interpretation. This passage still does not need to be read as inconsistent with Christian theology. Keith Ward argues that it is plausible to think that the Qur'an is condemning Arianism. Here, one might think that the condemnation is aimed toward those who worship Jesus as if he is another god, begotten from Allah. This is exactly the sort of concern Muhammad wanted to address as he rejected polytheistic traditions that saw gods begetting additional gods. There is to be no other being that is worshipped besides Allah.

What about those passages in the Qur'an, such as Surah 111:3, that tell us that God does not beget? Even if we can read Surah 9:30–31 in a way that is consistent with Jesus being identified with God, what are we to do with John explicitly stating that Jesus is the begotten Son of God? Christian theologians have generally understood language about God to be analogical rather than univocal. In this case, when Christians read passages like John 3:16, where Jesus is called the "only begotten Son," they don't literally think that Jesus is begotten in the same way that a human father begets a son. Now, Christians wouldn't take this completely equivocal either, such that the word begotten doesn't resemble how we predicate it to humans in our everyday experience. Rather, it is in between both univocal usage and equivocal usage. We can read the Qur'an's condemnation against God begetting as a condemnation of a univocal understanding of God begetting Jesus. So, when John affirms that Jesus is begotten and when the Qur'an condemns the view that Jesus is begotten, there can still be consistency. To put it in a way to appease analytic philosophers, we can say that God does not beget^1 but rather, God does beget^2.

Notice that the second part of my thesis for this chapter is simply that these religious traditions can be read in such a way as to render various religious traditions consistent (or nearby) with Nicene Christianity. Even if you don't find the reading offered here compelling, my thesis will succeed if you grant that it is remotely possible. After all, what I am after is logical consistency, not textual plausibility.

---

23. Abdullah Galardari, Personal Correspondence, December 3, 2022.

AN ANALYTIC CHRISTOLOGY OF RELIGIONS

Having said this, how are we to understand the Qur'an's rejection that God is a trinity? Surah 5:73 states that, "They have certainly disbelieved who say, 'Allāh is the third of three.' And there is no god except one God. And if they do not desist from what they are saying, there will surely afflict the disbelievers among them a painful punishment." Most Islamic commentators point out that the Qur'an is explicitly rejecting the Nicene doctrine of the Trinity. There are two problems with this, however. The doctrine of the Trinity does not endorse what we can call divine partialism. That is, the church has traditionally rejected the view that the Father, Son, and the Holy Spirit are individual pieces that make up Yahweh. Rather, the Father is identical to Yahweh, the Son is identical to Yahweh, and the Spirit is identical to Yahweh. Now, you might argue that this is contradictory since the Father is not the Son and the Son is not the Holy Spirit, but that is another topic for another day.[24] What is important here is that the church traditionally would reject what the Qur'an is rejecting as partialism isn't a faithful expression of the doctrine of the Trinity. Moreover, in verse 75, the Qur'an is rejecting a doctrine of the Trinity in which Mary is a member of it.[25] While this conceivably could have been a heresy going around during Muhammad's time, this again, isn't what Nicene Christianity endorses. The Nicene Christian, along with the faithful Muslim, can rejoice at the Qur'an's rejection of partialism and Mary being a member of the Trinity.

Now, all that I have said might clear the way for Muslims endorsing a high Christology, but what about the Qur'an's apparent denial that Jesus died on the cross? Surah 4:157 states the following:

> And because of their saying: We slew the Messiah, Jesus son of Mary, Allah's messenger—they slew him not nor crucified him, but it appeared so unto them; and lo! those who disagree concerning it are in doubt thereof; they have no knowledge thereof save pursuit of a conjecture; they slew him not for certain.[26]

Traditionally, Islamic theology has interpreted this passage to entail that Jesus was never actually crucified but rather he only appeared to be crucified. Typically, someone like Judas is seen as taking Jesus' place on the cross. But Surah 157 doesn't state this. Rather, it simply states that Jews who claimed to have crucified Jesus were wrong. They hadn't crucified Jesus but rather it

---

24. For resolving this issue, see Anderson, *Paradox in Christian Theology*.
25. See Reynold's *Qur'an and the Bible*, 208.
26. Pickthall translation.

PART II: THE MODEL

was made to simply look like it. Rather, as Christians believe, in a sense it was God who killed Jesus (Isa 53).

Ward takes a slightly different route around in interpreting this Surah:

> One could interpret this [Surah 157] as saying that Jesus did not pass into non-existence on the cross. He continued in conscious existence and ascended to God—a fact which Muslims confess. So, whereas the Jews thought they had consigned Jesus to the world of the dead at least until the final day of resurrection, they were mistaken in this belief . . .[27]

In this way, the Jews thought that they had killed Jesus and silenced his consciousness into the abyss, but this was far from what happened.

Finally, what should we make of proposition (3)? Can Christians really believe that Muhammad was God's prophet? Anna Bonta Moreland has recently argued that even Roman Catholics can believe that Muhammad was a prophet, at least in some sense.[28] To be clear, the Church teaches that Jesus is a complete and sufficient revelation. *Dominus Iesus* (*DI*) states this much as follows:

> The definitive and complete character of the revelation of Jesus Christ, the nature of Christian faith as compared with that of belief in other religions, the inspired nature of the books of Sacred Scripture, the personal unity between the Eternal Word and Jesus of Nazareth, the unity of the economy of the Incarnate Word and the Holy Spirit, the unicity and salvific universality of the mystery of Jesus Christ, the universal salvific mediation of the Church, the inseparability—while recognizing the distinction—of the kingdom of God, the kingdom of Christ, and the Church, and the subsistence of the one Church of Christ in the Catholic Church. (no. 4)

Yet, as Moreland points out, *DI* is completely consistent with thinking that the Qur'an is a private revelation.[29] In the Catholic tradition, while private revelation is never universally binding on all believers (and therefore not part of dogmatic theology), private revelation can still be interpreted as God granting prophetic utterances to his people. In this way, Catholics can believe that God raised up Muhammad to exhort the nations, especially those in the Arab world, that there is no God but Allah. However, God

---

27. Ward, *Religion and Revelation*, 182.
28. Moreland, "Qur'an and the doctrine of private revelation."
29. Moreland, "Qur'an and the doctrine of private revelation," 549.

doesn't see it necessary to force the Church to utilize the prophet's message for its dogmatic theology. Christ is sufficient for dogmatic theology.

Now, it could be the case that one's reading of the Qur'an is such that the Qur'an has to be read as a public revelation. If this is the case, it seems to me the Christian might think that while God was working with the Prophet Muhammad to bring about monotheism in the Middle East, Muhammad's interpretation of his private revelation is not infallible as the Christian Scripture is infallible. So, if there must be conflict, the revelation of Christ takes precedence. Having now argued that Islam can be interpreted to be doctrinally consistent with Christian belief, I now turn to examining the Advaita Vedanta tradition.

Advaita Vedanta

The Advaita Vedanta tradition is well known for endorsing claims such as "I and Brahman are one." Advaita Vedanta is often interpreted to be a radically monistic tradition. That is a tradition that has little room for ontological pluralism. Victoria Harrison helpfully puts the tradition's ontology in schematic form:

Layer 1: Absolute reality

Nirguṇa Brahman, Qualityless Brahman, Brahman/Ātman.

Layer 2:

Absolute reality seen through categories imposed by human thought Saguṇa Brahman, Brahman with qualities. Creator and governor of the world and a personal god (Īśvara, or Iswara).

Layer 3:
Conventional reality[30]

It is not hard to see why the Advaita Vedanta tradition is typically taken to be in conflict with Christianity. It seems that the Advaita Vedanta tradition denies the existence of a personal God, at least at the ultimate level of reality. Similarly, if there is only radical monism, then it seems the proponent is committed to pantheism or at best, panentheism. But must the Advaita Vedanta tradition be interpreted in such a way as to not have any room for

---

30. Harrison, *Eastern Philosophy*, 58.

PART II: THE MODEL

pluralism about objects? Contrary to standard interpretations of the tradition, Anantanand Rambachan argues that there is room "manyness."[31]

What's important for Rambachan is recognizing that at the ultimate layer of reality, there is only Brahman. In a private email correspondence, I asked Rambachan if the Advaita tradition could rightfully be seen through the lenses of Classical Theism. Specifically, can the Advaita proponent faithfully view God as ultimate reality, and yet argue that in some weaker sense, distinct objects also exist and participate in Brahman for their existence? Rambachan responded, "Your language of participation is an interesting possibility, if by participation you mean that nothing exists apart from brahman, nothing exists independently of brahman, and while things may have unique attributes etc., at the most fundamental of being or existence, all is brahman."[32] Ward also sees room for denying that creation is identical to Brahman: "What is the status of the individual mind, the agent and enjoyer, which we regard as the human soul? Sankara says, 'The Self does not exist . . . as an agent and enjoyer . . . the qualities of mind . . . are wrongly superimposed upon the Self.' But then it follows that the individual soul is in a very important respect not identical with Brahman."[33] Of course, the Classical Theist will rejoice in stating that God is ultimate reality, nothing exists apart from God, and nothing can exist independently of him. And since God is seen as Being or Existence itself, it is fair game to state that at the ultimate level of reality, all is God.

Now, you might wonder how one can be a Classical Theist and think that God isn't personal at the most ultimate layer of reality. In this case, must the Advaita Vedanta proponent think that God is impersonal? And are Classical Theists able to say that God is ultimately qualityless? Christopher Isherwood seems to think that the Advaita proponent must think that God is impersonal when he states, "Are there then two Gods—one the impersonal Brahman, the other the personal Iswara? No—for Brahman only appears as Iswara when viewed by the relative ignorance of maya. Iswara has the same degree of reality as maya has. God the Person is not Brahman in his ultimate nature."[34] But I'm not convinced that in

---

31. See Rambacan, *Hindu Theology of Liberation*, 64.

32. Anantanand Rambacan, Personal Correspondence, January 15, 2022.

33. Ward, *Religion and Revelation*, 151.

34. See the introduction to Śaṁkarācārya, *Shankara's Crest-Jewel of Discrimination*, 18.

the most literal sense Isherwood is right, at least if we are to believe that Brahman is truly qualityless.

To say that God is impersonal seems to put God into a genus. We are still using human categories to make sense of God. But at the ultimate layer, human categories do not correspond with God. Therefore, it might be better to say that God is neither personal nor impersonal, but rather God is completely Other. The Classical Theist is more than happy to concede that our language about God is only analogical. God doesn't literally possess properties since God is metaphysically simple. I, therefore, see no reason why the Classical Theist can't agree with the Advaita proponent about the various layers of reality. In this way, it seems plausible to me that the doctrine of Advaita Vedanta can be interpreted in such a way that it is consistent with the traditional theism of the Abrahamic traditions. As Ward compares Aquinas's conception of God, especially his doctrine of Divine Simplicity, with Shankara's conception of the qualityless Brahman, Ward states, "The deep unity of these views should be clear."[35] Ward goes on to say how that impersonal monism and personal dualism might seem at odds at first, at least if we take language about God to be univocal. As Ward points out, however, "it may be more appropriate . . . to regard such formulations as faltering attempts to express things that cannot be adequately described in available human concepts at all."[36]

But what shall we do with the idea that is clear in both the Upanishads and in Shankara's work, that "I am Brahman"? Shankara interestingly enough cites the following Bhagavad-Gita's passage to make sense of how our identity at the fundamental level is Brahman:

> Sri Krishna, the incarnate Lord, who knows the secret of all truths, says in the Gita: "Although I am not within any creature, all creatures exist within me. I do not mean that they exist with me physically. My Being sustains all creatures and brings them to birth, but has no physical contact with them."[37]

Interestingly enough, in the Thomistic tradition creatures are said to participate in God without it being the case that "God is physically them." If what the Advaita Vedanta proponent means by "I am Brahman" is simply that there is a sense in which our ego is not ultimate and behind the ego

---

35. Ward, *Religion and Revelation*, 153.
36. Ward, *Religion and Revelation*, 153.
37. Śaṁkarācārya, *Shankara's Crest-Jewel of Discrimination*, 70–71.

is ultimately pure consciousness, then the Christian can agree. As Brian Davies points out, this view is well grounded in the Christian tradition:

> God is ultimate reality. And Catherine of Sienna, whose thinking is governed by the notion of God as source of everything, repeatedly says that only God is and she herself is not. In similar vein, [Jonathan] Edwards explains that creatures are, in a sense, "empty." By "creature being thus wholly and universally dependent on God," writes Edwards, "it appears that the creature is nothing, and that God is all."[38]

Whether human beings are "empty" should be further explored and we will do that by engaging Buddhist philosophy below.

Buddhism[39]

The Buddhist philosopher Jay Garfield summarizes a contemporary and minimalist interpretation of Buddhism as follows:

> Suffering (*dukkha*) or discontent is ubiquitous in the world . . .
>
> The origin of dukkha is in primal confusion about the fundamental nature of reality, and so its cure is at bottom a reorientation toward ontology and an awakening (*bodhi*) to the actual nature of existence.
>
> All phenomena are impermanent (***anitya***), interdependent (***pratītya-samutpāda***) and have no intrinsic nature (***śūnya***) . . .
>
> Fundamental confusion is to take phenomena, including preeminently oneself, to be permanent, independent and to have an essence or intrinsic nature (*svabhāva*).
>
> The elimination (*nirvāṇa*), or at least the substantial reduction of dukkha through such reorientation, is possible.
>
> An ethically appropriate orientation toward the world is characterized by the cultivation of *mudita* (an attitude of rejoicing in the welfare and goodness of others, of *mettā* beneficence toward others, and especially of *karuṇā* (commitment to act for the welfare of sentient beings).[40]

---

38. Davies, "Letter from America," 373.

39. I make these same points, though more thoroughly, in McNabb and Baldwin, *Classical Theism and Buddhism*.

40. Garfield, *Engaging Buddhism*, 2.

The highlighted portion is what I take to be most in tension with Christian doctrine. At the heart of Buddhism are the interdependence and impermanent theses. Roughly the idea of interdependence is that all things, ontologically, are dependent on one another.

For example, if X is a thing, then its existence (both causally and conceptually) would depend on Y, and Y would depend on Z, and so on. David Burton puts this thesis as follows, "all entities have a dependently arisen and conceptually constructed existence . . ."[41] Garfield puts it slightly differently when he states, "All events in time, all Buddhist philosophers agree, occur in dependence to prior causes and conditions, and all states of affairs cease when the cause and conditions that are necessary for their occurrence cease."[42]

Impermanence on the other hand is the thesis that all things are in constant state of change. Usually, a radical interpretation of Leibniz's law of identity is applied. Anytime there is subtle change with respect to some object O, O no longer exists, but rather a new object, O2, comes into existence. Any new property gained, or any property lost, while it might seem subtle, constitutes a new identity. Endorsing these two theses leads to the doctrine that things ultimately lack *svabhāva*, or an intrinsic nature.

Now, you might be wondering how these theses are consistent with theism, or specifically, Christianity. I concede that if one primarily construes God as a thing, that is, simply as an additional object in the universe, then one would have to accept the absurd view that the God who existed yesterday is not the same God who exists today, and will not be the same God who exists tomorrow. Similarly, one would have to be committed to the view that God is dependent on his creation as all things are interdependent. These are unacceptable conclusions for theists, especially of the Nicene Christian stripe. But as noted in the Introduction of this volume, for this book's purposes, Classical Theism is assumed. God is not another entity in the universe or simply one existent thing among many other existent things. As the neo-Platonic tradition puts it, God is nothing. Rather, God is Existence itself.

It's at least not *prima facie* obvious to me why a Christian can't endorse the aforementioned theses. Recall again, Brian Davies is under the impression that both Jonathan Edwards and Catherine of Sienna both affirmed the interdependence thesis:

41. Burton, *Emptiness Appraised*, 36.
42. Garfield, *Engaging Buddhism*, 27.

God is ultimate reality. And Catherine of Sienna, whose thinking is governed by the notion of God as source of everything, repeatedly says that only God is and she herself is not. In similar vein, Edwards explains that creatures are, in a sense, "empty." By "creature being thus wholly and universally dependent on God," writes Edwards, "it appears that the creature is nothing, and that God is all."[43]

Similarly, Edwards seems to also endorse the impermanence thesis and has his own way of making sense of personal identity and eschatological judgement.[44] For those interested in how Buddhist religious experience and Buddhist soteriological beliefs can be consistent with Christian views, see my volume with Erik Baldwin, *Classical Theism and Buddhism*.[45]

Ward has a different approach to making sense of how Buddhism and theism could be considered consistent. Ward appeals to the permanent nature of Nirvana that he describes from the *Dhammapada*, as peaceful and infinite joy. Ward seems to think that Nirvana can be understood as pure consciousness. Ward goes on to describe what some Buddhists refer to as the cosmic Body of the Buddha as a possible link for making sense of there being an eternal or permanent feature in reality.[46] As for now, I will take it that I have made plausible the second part of my thesis for this chapter, namely that other serious religious traditions can be interpreted as doctrinally consistent with (or something nearby) the Christian Nicene tradition.

Conclusion

Why is it important to establish my theses for this chapter? Why take a whole chapter in a book on the theology of evangelism to discuss a christological view of other world religions? A Christology of religions is extremely practical for evangelism. How should we evangelize other faiths? I hope my thoughts on this question have been made clear. If other religious traditions contain plenty of truth and can be interpreted as an attempt to know the same Divine reality, the evangelist should concede as much as possible to those who are not, at least explicitly, believers. That is, the focus shouldn't be on religious disagreement (though this may have its place). Rather, the focus should be on showing how the religious tradition in question can be

---

43. Brian Davies, "Letter from America," 373.
44. See chapter 1 of McNabb and Baldwin, *Classical Theism and Buddhism*.
45. McNabb and Baldwin, *Classical Theism and Buddhism*.
46. Ward, *Religion and Revelation*, 163–67.

seen as consistent with the core doctrines of Christianity, as well as proclaiming the fullness of the gospel message. Now, one might wonder why we should evangelize if we can be optimistic about the number of those who will ultimately partake in the beatific vision. Why should we approach evangelism with urgency? I now turn to answer these questions and ethical concerns about evangelism in the last two chapters.

Part III

The Objections

5

Evangelism as Epistemic and Cultural Violence

EVANGELISM, IF IT CONSISTS of anything, consists of proclaiming the kerygma of the Christian faith. That is, evangelism consists of proclaiming the death, burial, and resurrection of Christ in hope that individuals will come to fully participate in the church and her sacraments. As the reader is well aware, this book presupposes that the propositions of Nicene Christianity are true. So, again, I'm interested in engaging objections to the practice of evangelism that assume the truth of Christianity. You might wonder if Christianity is true, how could anyone object to the practice of evangelism? Shouldn't coming into full communion with Christ's holy church and receiving her sacraments as a means of salvation takes precedence over all other concerns? You would think, but alas, that is not the case. In what follows, I will engage a series of objections. I turn to the claim that it is simply "obviously wrong" that evangelism should be practiced.

The Obviously Wrong Objection

Perhaps our objector argues that evangelism is simply "obviously" wrong. Maybe it is such that S has an extraordinarily strong seeming that leads her to believe this way. Or perhaps S even claims that it is an analytic truth. In the same way we see that bachelors could never be married, we can also see that it is always wrong to try to convert others to a different faith.

PART III: THE OBJECTIONS

I must confess that this objection has never moved me in the slightest. I mean, the traditional world religions have always had members evangelize or promote their religious thinking to others in an attempt to create converts. Whether it be a guru, apostle, or Old Testament prophets, there is a long history of attempting to get converts to one's religious views. It is interesting to note that for the vast majority of religious proponents over thousands of years, few if any thought evangelism was simply "obviously wrong." This way of thinking seems to gain popularity post-World War II. I think there is something to be said here.

Now, I imagine one rejoinder could be that slavery has also been seen as morally acceptable in many religious traditions, nonetheless, we (hopefully) think that slavery is obviously wrong. For example, the Old Testament and the Qur'an have rules to regulate slavery and the New Testament encourages slaves to obey their masters. If slavery didn't seem so obviously bad to many religious persons then, it nonetheless doesn't follow that it still isn't, objectively speaking, obviously wrong (at least, for those who have properly functioning cognitive faculties and who are in the right epistemic environment).

I do think there are important points for our consideration. First, it isn't such that slavery is given a glorious endorsement by the Abrahamic traditions. There are rules that make it obligatory to set slaves free in the Old Testament. There is also encouragement in both the Qur'an and the New Testament to free slaves. In fact, it is typically argued that if Paul didn't see the fullness of the eschaton occurring immediately, he might have forbidden slavery wholesale. Nonetheless, slavery being wrong didn't just become unacceptable to all religious persons. There is a history in the Christian faith of opposing the practice and this picks up especially upon the discovery of the New World.[1]

Nonetheless, the "obviously wrong" objection is hard to square with the Great Commission (i.e., Matthew 28) and the practice of the apostles in the book of Acts. If Nicene Christianity is true, then it seems unlikely that Jesus was wrong for giving the Great Commission. Similarly, it's unlikely that the apostles practiced something immoral all throughout the book of Acts, especially given that they likely saw their witnessing as something essential to their faith.

Nonetheless, if I were a liberal scholar, I might accept the Nicene Creed, and yet reject that the Great Commission was given by the historical

---

1. For a look at the progression, see Noonan, *Church that Can and Cannot Change*.

Jesus. Of course, if I wanted to argue for its historicity, I could argue that Jesus was simply commanding his apostles to teach the world to love God and their neighbor. *Contra* how evangelism is normally understood, the call to evangelize is nothing more than visiting the sick and imprisoned, feeding the poor, and telling others to do likewise (Matt 25:37–46).

Of course, there is the whole baptizing the nations in the name of the Trinity thing, which seems to presuppose that there are at least some doctrinal commitments that need to be expressed as one attempts to persuade others to be baptized and believe in the triune God. Nonetheless, let's assume for argument's sake that the Nicene Christian we are engaging interprets the Great Commission only in light of Matthew 25:37–46 and without doctrinal commitments. Perhaps there is logical space for this approach, but this all seems rather implausible.

More to our point, however, I'm still at a loss for how the practice of evangelism, is supposed to seem so obviously wrong. Perhaps there is an equivocation going on when we are discussing evangelism. The Catholic tradition draws a distinction between proselytizing and evangelism. The former has connotations of manipulating people into the faith. One can do this by threat or by taking advantage of the sick and uneducated. Proselytizing often is understood to treat people as only a means to an end rather than an end in themselves. Evangelism, on the other hand, represents a practice of lovingly proclaiming the death, burial, and resurrection of Christ in hope that it draws people to a closer relationship to Christ.

The United States Council for Catholic Bishop's published an article by Fr. Leo Walsh that draws the distinction between proselytism and evangelism in further detail.[2] Fr. Walsh quotes from part of "Towards a Common Witness" to help elucidate the distinction. According to this interdenominational document, proselytism includes the following:

> Making unjust or uncharitable
> references to other churches' beliefs
> and practices and even ridiculing them.
> Comparing two Christian
> communities by emphasizing the
> achievements and ideals of one, and the
> weaknesses and practical problems of
> the other.

---

2. Walsh, "Proselytism and Evangelization," 3.

> Employing any kind of physical violence, moral compulsion and psychological pressure, e.g., the use of certain advertising techniques in mass media that might bring undue pressure on readers/viewers.
>
> Using political, social and economic power as a means of winning new members for one's own church.
>
> Extending explicit or implicit offers of education, health care, or material inducements or using financial resources with the intent of making converts.
>
> Manipulative attitudes and practices that exploit people's needs, weaknesses or lack of education . . .[3]

The Methodist scholar Bryan Stone draws this distinction as well when he connects proselytizing with attempting to make converts and connects evangelism simply with the practice of being a faithful witness to the Christian faith.[4] So maybe the Obvious Objection pertains more to something like proselytizing than the practice of evangelism.

While I want to reject the practice of proselytizing, at least if proselytizing entails manipulation or coercion, it isn't obvious to me why proselytizing is wrong if all we mean by that is an attempt to obtain converts to a position that we think is true. That's how Elmer John Thiessen defines it when he states that when using the word, he uses it in "neutral sense to describe any activity that attempts to bring about a conversion."[5] Thus, we can draw a further distinction between proselytizing in this mundane sense of the term, say proselytizing^1, and, in the more coercive sense of the term, say proselytizing^2. Why is proselytizing^1 so bad?

I'm a philosophy professor. In my discipline, we go to academic conferences and deliver papers that usually attempt to convert the audience

---

3. World Council of Churches, "Towards a Common Witness," https://www.oikoumene.org/resources/documents/towards-common-witness.

4. Stone, *Evangelism After Pluralism*, 17.

5. Thiessen, *Ethics of Evangelism*, 27.

from one way of thinking to another. For example, I might present on a paper arguing for a proper functionalist theory of warrant. My goal would be to defend the theory or put forth a compelling reason for my audience to reconsider the theory. Is this wrong? Doubtful.

Maybe it is not wrong because I am presenting the paper in front of other academics, but if I were to present in front of philosophical laymen, then that would be wrong. But surely, this can't be the case or else teaching students would be wrong! Perhaps teaching "facts" that everyone agrees on is permissible but we shouldn't teach a view as "true" if reasonable people disagree with the view. But for every ten philosophers, there are at least eleven different views endorsed. There are philosophers who argue that infants are not persons,[6] that we are in a computer simulation,[7] that we can have sex with nonrational animals,[8] and there are even philosophers who argue that we can't have knowledge.[9] Surely, we can teach these views as false in the classroom, or their rival views as true. Again, what is so wrong with proseyltism[1]?

Epistemic Violence Objection

Samuel Lebens has recently published a fascinating article that argues that proselytism can be an act of epistemic violence.[10] Lebens defines proselytism as an act that persuades "a person outside of your faith community to commit to your religion."[11] Lebens goes on to argue that religion typically roots an individual in a particular epistemic community. Religion enables the agent to access various sources of potential knowledge. Such sources can include Scripture, tradition, and a living community. To rip someone out of their epistemic context into another can do damage to the religious agent's way of thinking and knowing. We can imagine in some cases that the radical departure from one religious' tradition might do more damage than good. It might cause the agent to love God less or to be a worse person more generally. In some cases, it might cause families to divide and fall apart.

6. Tooely, "Abortion and Infanticide."
7. Bostrom, "Are You Living in a Computer Simulation?"
8. Singer, "Heavy petting."
9. Unger, "Defense of Skepticism."
10. Lebens, "Proselytism as Epistemic Violence."
11. Lebens, "Proselytism as Epistemic Violence," 376.

Now, one response is to argue that the material or finite goods one loses in this life simply do not compare to the infinite reward one gains by conversion. So, even if trying to get a subject to convert leads to material loss, it at least leads to eternal gain. We should still, then, aim to get people to convert. Lebens isn't convinced by this line of reasoning. Lebens endorses the following principle:

> (A) No good and reasonable God could possibly condition salvation upon a person doing or believing that which is practically irrational for them to do or believe, so long as they're not to blame for being in a state that renders that action or belief irrational.[12]

Lebens argues that a reasonable and good God would never make a subject's salvation dependent on the subject disconnecting from her epistemic roots (i.e., doing something practically irrational), at least if she is not culpable for not disconnecting to begin with. Lebens goes on to argue that disconnecting from one's epistemic roots requires a significant burden of proof. That is, a subject would need to have overwhelming proof that another religious tradition is true in order for her to be culpable for not converting. While theism more broadly construed might have overwhelming evidence that can support it, Lebens seems skeptical about the prospects of a specific monotheistic tradition being in the same position.

Ultimately, this is why proselytism in philosophy is permissible while proselytism with respect to religion is not. Religion centers an epistemic agent. It gives her a community. It gives her various sources from which she will utilize to discover the world. I can get you to try to change your view about an epistemic theory, but that won't have a devastating impact on you. Changing your religion has an existential risk. Lebens thinks that proselytism is epistemic violence; and it is violence that at least in some cases is simply not justified.

Now, what can we say in response to Lebens? Well, first, one could argue that Lebens's understanding of God is too anthropomorphic. For Lebens, God seems to be a moral agent and person. It is as if we can understand what it means for God to be good and reasonable in a univocal way since Lebens seems to think we can predict what God would or would not do. Again, the reader might recall that, for sake of argument, this book assumes that Classical Theism is true. Lebens's contention that a good and reasonable God wouldn't damn a subject to hell for not wanting

---

12. Lebens, "Proselytism as Epistemic Violence," 388.

to cut off their epistemic roots ought to be seen as suspect. We are simply not in the position to know what God would do in this situation, at least not without revelation.

Second, one might follow Richard Swinburne and argue that there is overwhelming evidence for Christianity. Swinburne famously puts the probability that Jesus rose from the dead at a staggering .97.[13] One then might concede Lebens's general argument but disagree that it applies to Christian belief since Christian belief can meet his evidentialist demands.

Third, one could run a reductio to Lebens' position. How would Lebens have us treat political disagreements? Let's say there are two candidates running on two radically different platforms. Let's say that Joe is card-carrying member of a political party that advocates for policies that will ultimately harm the society. Nonetheless, the party has given Joe an important intellectual formation. There are authorities within his party that guide him, there are *de facto* Scriptures that party members work from to make their political decisions, and of course, in this case, all of Joe's friends are card-carrying members of the party. In fact, we can even stipulate that his marriage depends on him being a party member. Would it be wrong for Ron, a member of the other party, to try convince Joe to cut his epistemic roots, even if there wasn't overwhelming evidence (we can say Ron's rational credence is .85) that Joe's party is destructive? Again, not likely.

But maybe all this objecting to Lebens is unnecessary. In his paper, Lebens argues that proselytism to a general audience is permissible.[14] For example, I can write a book arguing for why Christianity is true. Similarly, I can post videos to social media in an attempt to convert my audience. Perhaps Lebens is open to a form of proselytism where S^1 can share her religious beliefs with S^2, and even make a plausible case for them in hope that S^2 becomes a Christian. At least, if S^1 takes a more generalized approach with S^2. What Lebens seems to be against, rather, is S^1 making S^2's conversion her focal point, where S^1 is doing all that she can do to get S^2 to cut off his epistemic roots, when it seems, ultimately, harmful. We can get rid of the word *proselytism*, however, and replace it with what Catholics simply call it, "evangelization." Once S^1 faithfully shares the gospel with S^2 in an abstract or generalized way, and, S^1 answers any objections given by S^2, S^1 has fulfilled her duty to proclaim the gospel and she can now rest as she allows the Spirit to operate. If this isn't objectionable, then it seems

---

13. Swinburne, *Resurrection of God Incarnate*.
14. Lebens, "Proselytism as Epistemic Violence," 378.

PART III: THE OBJECTIONS

Lebens's targeted audience is a different one then the one I have in mind. Our disagreement only needs to be in name only.

Colonialism Objection

Perhaps our objector is inclined to dismiss the practice of evangelism, not because it is an instance of epistemic violence, but because it is an instance of colonialism. One might even go so far as to argue that Christian missions is a form of cultural genocide. While I am sure there are as many definitions of colonialism as there are actual cultures, for our purposes we can work off the following definition: Colonialism is the act of subjugating one culture to another.[15]

One worry is that colonialism is intrinsically wrong. And if evangelism is a form of colonialism, it could never be the case that God calls the church to evangelize. The church has simply been in the wrong for promoting such a practice.

What can we say on behalf of the evangelist? For starters, it isn't clear to me that colonialism is inherently wrong. For example, was it wrong to dismantle the Nazi government in the 1940s, and for some time, have other countries run its government until things got situated? I imagine few would object to this. But yet, in this case, you have the subjection of one culture to another.

According to orthodox Christian theology, Jesus the Christ is coming back to earth. Now, without getting in a debate about whether Christ is already reigning on earth (he is), we can all agree that he will be. Christian theology has it as such that all nations will submit to the reign of Christ (1 Cor 15). In some sense, all cultures will be subjected to a human person of another culture, Jesus. Again, this doesn't seem morally problematic.

Perhaps the objector thinks it is permissible for some parts of culture to be subjected to another, but it is the wholesale rejection or change from one culture to another that is deeply problematic. But it is important to point out that the church doesn't advocate for a complete rejection of non-Christian culture. As we discussed in chapter 4, *Ad Gentes* informs us that God reveals truths in other religious and cultural settings:

> But whatever truth and grace are to be found among the nations,
> as a sort of secret presence of God, He frees from all taint of evil

15. This definition is essentially the definition advocated by Kohn and Reddy, "Colonialism," https://plato.stanford.edu/entries/colonialism/.

and restores to Christ its maker, who overthrows the devil's domain and wards off the manifold malice of vice. And so, whatever good is found to be sown in the hearts and minds of men, or in the rites and cultures peculiar to various peoples, not only is not lost, but is healed, uplifted, and perfected for the glory of God, the shame of the demon, and the bliss of men.

In fact, it is through the gospel that the rites, customs, and rituals found in other non-Christian traditions, reach their ultimate fulfillment. Generally speaking, the church has no interest in rejecting customs of other traditions. We can, again, illustrate this clearly by looking at how the Jesuits evangelized Eastern Asia. The church sees beauty and truth in the customs of others. Now, of course there might be some customs that are inconsistent with the gospel, for example, burning alive widows with their deceased husbands, or owning slaves. But surely there is nothing objectionable in changing these practices. So, again, we are left with the question: What is wrong with evangelism?

Political Objection

Maybe there is a political concern. If the state for example supports the right for conflicting religious groups to evangelize each other, chaos would ensue and the common good would be compromised. We all know the history of religious intolerance. Christians and Muslims have gone to war with one another on numerous occasions. Even within Christendom, Catholics and Protestants have had their fair share of bloody battles. Even if evangelism isn't intrinsically wrong, it seems like the state has a vested interest to be neutral with respect to religion, and therefore, discourage evangelism as a practice.

But how is this staying neutral? In this example, isn't the state *de facto* favoring atheism or whatever secular philosophy seems to be in place at the time? If one were to truly be neutral, it seems like the state would have to minimize its involvement in religious practice and influence wholesale. Of course, the idea that the state needs to be neutral is a product of liberal (and more recently Rawlsian) ideology. For most of Christendom, however, liberalism was not the Church's position. Instead, the Church thought that the state ought to favor true religion.[16] It isn't at all clear to me that the Christian needs to endorse liberalism. There are even recent sophisticated objections

16. See chapter 2 of Vallier's *All Kingdoms of the World*; Jones, *Two Cities*.

to various forms of liberalism that need to still be addressed.[17] All this to say, I don't think state neutrality is going to get us anywhere. So, what is wrong with the practice of evangelism? Answer: Nothing.

---

17. Vallier, *Liberal Politics and Public Faith*; Vallier, "Convergence and Consensus"; McNabb, *God and Political Theory*; McNabb, "Against the Access Requirement"; Deneen, *Why Liberalism Failed*.

6

It's the End: A Short Reflection on How Many Will Be Saved

LET'S TAKE A MOMENT and reflect on our journey. In chapter 1, I started this volume by clarifying the nature of the gospel, defending its historicity, and arguing that all baptized Christians are called to evangelize. In chapter 2, I argued that not only do Catholics and Protestants believe in the same gospel, but that the Catholic conception of justification is consistent with many Protestant creeds and contemporary Protestant scholarship.

I then moved to develop a model for evangelism. In chapter 3, I surveyed important evangelists and missionaries in the church's history. Taking insights from the lives of the saints, I developed what I called the TSM. In chapter 4, I further added to TSM by way of developing a Christology of religions. This, I argued, should shape our method of evangelism.

After developing the TSM, I looked at various contemporary ethical objections to evangelism. Having argued that the objections are all found wanting, we now find ourselves in this last chapter. This chapter is in a sense, another chapter engaging an objection to evangelism. Except in this case, I want to engage an objection to evangelism that is theological in nature.

In Protestant and Orthodox circles, partly due to the influence of theologians such as David Hart[1] and Robin Parry,[2] universalism is all the rage. While Catholics are not allowed to accept universalism full-stop, theologians

---

1. Hart, *That All Shall Be Saved*.
2. MacDonald (pseudonym), *Evangelical Universalist*.

PART III: THE OBJECTIONS

like Hans Urs Von Balthasar have argued that Catholics can at least have a reasonable hope for universalism. One might ask, "If universalism is true, why should we approach evangelism with urgency?"

There are many ways one can respond. Firstly, one might argue on pure deontological grounds that we ought to evangelize since God has commanded his church to evangelize. As long as God binds his church to teach the nations all that he has commanded, the church is obligated to share the gospel. Secondly, belief in the gospel brings about real world reconciliation. The gospel reconciles families, people groups, countries, and religious communities. The gospel brings mental sanity and spiritual clarity. The gospel also radically changes lives for the better. These are pretty important goods! We ought not to deprive our fellow humans the opportunity to obtain these goods in the here and now.

Thirdly, and more to the point for our purposes, I'm sympathetic to Balthasar's primary point in *Dare We Hope That All Men Be Saved?*. Much of theology is paradox. As I have argued elsewhere,[3] assuming that God is not a being among other beings but is rather Being itself, our language about God is at best, analogical. We should then expect there to be unarticulated equivocations when we speak of God. When I look at Scripture, I see passages that could plausibly be used to support the universalism thesis, such as the following:

> Colossians 1:20 . . . and through him to reconcile to himself all things, whether on earth or in heaven, making peace by the blood of his cross.

> Romans 5:18 Therefore, as one trespass led to condemnation for all men, so one act of righteousness leads to justification and life for all men.

> 1 John 2:2 He is the propitiation for our sins, and not for ours only but also for the sins of the whole world.

Similarly, there are passages that clearly paint a bleak picture of how many will be saved, such as the following:

> Matthew 7:13–14 Enter by the narrow gate. For the gate is wide and the way is easy that leads to destruction, and those who enter by it are many. For the gate is narrow and the way is hard that leads to life, and those who find it are few.

---

3. Balthasar, *Dare We Hope That All Men Be Saved?*

> Revelation 20:13-15 And the sea gave up the dead who were in it, Death and Hades gave up the dead who were in them, and they were judged, each one of them, according to what they had done. Then Death and Hades were thrown into the lake of fire. This is the second death, the lake of fire.
>
> Jude 1:3-4 Beloved, although I was very eager to write to you about our common salvation, I found it necessary to write appealing to you to contend for the faith that was once for all delivered to the saints. ⁴ For certain people have crept in unnoticed who long ago were designated for this condemnation, ungodly people, who pervert the grace of our God into sensuality and deny our only Master and Lord, Jesus Christ.

How can these passages be reconciled? Of course, I think they can be. But until the infallible magisterium makes a declaration, I'm inclined to think it is beyond my ken to figure out exactly to square these passages. This might be by design. God might want us to live with tension with respect to having hope that all are saved, and yet having an understanding that there is a real possibility that most will ultimately be lost.

But if I am honest, I expect many more to be saved than lost. In my Catholic tradition, there are three conditions that need to be in place for mortal sin to be committed. The act must be grave, the grave act must be taken with full knowledge that it is a grave act,[4] and the grave act can't be sufficiently coerced. It is only when these conditions are met that one performs an unfaithful act to God. I'm hopeful that many who perform grave acts are missing either the knowledge or freedom requirements for mortal sin. In this way, I follow Pope Benedict's expectations:

> There can be people who have totally destroyed their desire for truth and readiness to love, people for whom everything has become a lie, people who have lived for hatred and have suppressed all love within themselves. This is a terrifying thought, but alarming profiles of this type can be seen in certain figures of our own history. In such people all would be beyond remedy and the destruction of good would be irrevocable: this is what we mean by the word *Hell*. On the other hand there can be people who are utterly pure, completely permeated by God, and thus fully open to their neighbours—people for whom communion with God even now gives direction to their entire being and whose journey towards God only brings to fulfilment what they already are.

---

4. There is of course, vincible ignorance that could negate this requirement from having to be met.

46. Yet we know from experience that neither case is normal in human life. For the great majority of people—we may suppose—there remains in the depths of their being an ultimate interior openness to truth, to love, to God. In the concrete choices of life, however, it is covered over by ever new compromises with evil—much filth covers purity, but the thirst for purity remains and it still constantly re-emerges from all that is base and remains present in the soul. What happens to such individuals when they appear before the Judge? Will all the impurity they have amassed through life suddenly cease to matter? What else might occur? Saint Paul, in his *First Letter to the Corinthians*, gives us an idea of the differing impact of God's judgement according to each person's particular circumstances. He does this using images which in some way try to express the invisible, without it being possible for us to conceptualize these images—simply because we can neither see into the world beyond death nor do we have any experience of it. Paul begins by saying that Christian life is built upon a common foundation: Jesus Christ. This foundation endures. If we have stood firm on this foundation and built our life upon it, we know that it cannot be taken away from us even in death. Then Paul continues: "Now if any one builds on the foundation with gold, silver, precious stones, wood, hay, straw—each man's work will become manifest; for the Day will disclose it, because it will be revealed with fire, and the fire will test what sort of work each one has done. If the work which any man has built on the foundation survives, he will receive a reward. If any man's work is burned up, he will suffer loss, though he himself will be saved, but only as through fire" (1 Cor 3:12–15). In this text, it is in any case evident that our salvation can take different forms, that some of what is built may be burned down, that in order to be saved we personally have to pass through "fire" so as to become fully open to receiving God and able to take our place at the table of the eternal marriage-feast.[5]

Nonetheless, it isn't our place to know, not with any certainty. And until we see Christ face to face, we will lack that certainty. Until then, it seems safer to wager in favor of those who reject universalism or its close cousins. Following Pascal,[6] we can reason in the following way:

If universalism is true and we act as if universalism is true, what is gained? Aren't the goods discussed earlier in this chapter important enough that evangelism should still be seen as urgent? I don't think we have any reason to significantly modify how we allocate the church's resources.

5. Pope Benedict, *Spe Salvi*.
6. Pascal, *Pensées*.

If universalism is true and we act like universalism is false, again what do we lose? We decreased spiritual suffering and fostered genuine reconciliation between families and people groups. There seems to be a net positive.

If universalism turns out to be false and we acted as if universalism is true, what do we lose? While, plausibly, we should still see evangelism as urgent even if we believe in universalism, it seems likely that many would become lax in their evangelism efforts and in their giving to missions. Likely, we would be losing eternal life for many souls.

Finally, if universalism is false, and we acted as if universalism is false, we lose nothing.

The cost for assuming universalism is true, and universalism turning out to be false, is simply too high. It is simply not worth the risk. There is a theory in contemporary epistemology known as contextualism.[7] The view is roughly this: The context we are in could change whether we are said to know some proposition. This could be due to epistemic or non-epistemic factors. For example, in a context where you want to get to the movies on time, a simple look at the movie theater schedule might suffice. In a context where your life depends on getting to the movie theater on time, you might need something more than a quick reflection. In this case, with a lot riding on universalism being true, the context could make it impossible for knowing that universalism is true.

There is another angle one can take to arrive at the same destination. It has to do with accepting what epistemologists call pragmatic encroachment. Roughly, pragmatic encroachment's thesis is that non-epistemic factors, such as pragmatic considerations, are relevant for determining whether or not knowledge can be had.[8] Again, in this case, it might be that it is simply not practical to believe universalism is true. Given the practical loss for believing universalism is so significant, universalism might be a belief that can never count as knowledge.

For these reasons among many others, it is clear to me that the church should see her mission as urgent. She simply has too much to lose. It is my hope that this project is the start of a new larger project in analytic theology. I pray that many more works come forth discussing the theology of the church's "urgent" mission.

---

7. Black, "Contextualism in Epistemology."

8. For an argument that atheism can never be justified for similar reasons, see Benton, "Pragmatic Encroachment and Theistic Knowledge."

Appendix

Approaches to Street Evangelism

WE ALL KNOW THE common trope of the local street preacher. There is some older gentlemen preaching to no one in the middle of a street while he holds either a sign warning of damnation or a King James Bible. Can street evangelism be done in a way that doesn't come across as alienating and obnoxious? Before becoming a philosopher, I spent many years doing street evangelism, mostly as a Reformed Baptist minister. In some sense, this is part of my motivation for writing this book. Even to this day, I still try to do occasional street evangelism. It is a practice found firmly within the Christian tradition. The apostles did it, the medieval Church did it, and as we saw in chapter 3, Catholics and Protestants revived the practice in the eighteenth and nineteenth centuries. Street evangelism is being done to this very day.

One could of course write a whole volume on street evangelism and whether or not it is a permissible or a practical practice for today. One weakness of this volume is that, while I clarify what evangelism is as a practice and defend the view that all are called to evangelize, I never developed in detail the best modes for accomplishing the task. I'll leave that task to someone else. As for now, I'd like to sketch out various approaches that one could take if they were interested in continuing the practice today.

Approach one: Find a populated area. Set a desk up with tracts and rosaries (maybe even cookies). Ask people walking by if they would like a rosary or a cross. Then ask them about their views on God and start off a conversation by listening to the views and worries that are expressed. You can figure out whether you need to present the gospel next or answer an objection or concern. This approach seems to be the preferred method of St. Paul Street Evangelization ministry.

Approach two: Go to a college campus with an erase board. Have some catchy or thought-provoking question on the erase board and lovingly ask people that walk by what they think about the question. For example, one might write down something like, "Science and Religion are Compatible, Change my Mind." You can then talk to the students and their views on religion, do apologetics if necessary, and ultimately share the gospel.

Approach three: Find a populated area. Start open air preaching arguments for the existence of God. You could start shouting out the premises of the Kalam cosmological argument for example. The goal is to try to get people to ask questions or object to you. The second someone stops to talk with you, you will have a large crowd. People are hungry to get answers and to hear various perspectives on the God question. After answering questions, you can then share the gospel.

Bibliography

Abraham, William. *Divine Agency and Divine Action*. Vol 1. New York: Oxford University Press, 2017.
———. *The Logic of Evangelism*. Grand Rapids: Eerdmans, 1989.
Allison, Dale. *Constructing Jesus: Memory, Imagination, and History*. Grand Rapids: Baker Academic, 2013.
———. *The Historical Christ and the Theological Jesus*. Grand Rapids: Eerdmans, 2009.
———. *The Resurrection of Jesus: Apologetics, Polemics, and History*. London: T. & T. Clark, 2021.
Anderson, James. *Paradox in Christian Theology*. Milton Keynes: Paternoster, 2007.
Balthasar, Hans Urs Von. *Dare We Hope That All Men Be Saved?* San Francisco: Ignatius, 2014.
Baldwin, Erik, and Tyler Dalton McNabb. *Plantingian Religious Epistemology and World Religions*. Lanham, MD: Lexington, 2018.
Barber, Michael. *The Historical Jesus and the Temple: Memory, Methodology, and the Gospel of Matthew*. Cambridge: Cambridge University Press, 2023.
Bauckham, Richard. *Jesus and the Eyewitnesses: The Gospels as Eyewitness Testimony*. Grand Rapids: Eerdmans, 2007.
Benton, Matthew. "Pragmatic Encroachment and Theistic Knowledge." In *Knowledge, Belief, and God: New Insights in Religious Epistemology*, edited by Matthew Benton, John Hawthorne, and Dani Rabinowitz, 267–77. Oxford: Oxford University Press, 2018.
Bermejo-Rubio, Fernando. "Changing Methods, Disturbing Material. Should the Criteria of Embarrassment be Dismissed in Jesus Research?" *Revue des Etudes Juives* 175 (2016) 1–25.
Bird, Michael. *Evangelical Theology*. Kindle ed. Grand Rapids: Zondervan, 2020.
Black, Tim. "Contextualism in Epistemology." *Internet Encyclopedia of Philosophy*. https://iep.utm.edu/contextualism-in-epistemology/.
Bonaventure. *The Life of Saint Francis of Assisi*. Gastonia: Tan, 2010.

BIBLIOGRAPHY

Bostrom, Nick. "Are You Living in a Computer Simulation?" *Philosophical Quarterly* 53 (2003) 243–55.

Burton, David. *Emptiness Appraised: A Critical Study of Nāgārjuna's Philosophy*. London: Routledge, 2015.

Davies, Brian. "Letter from America." *New Black Friars* (2007) 371–84.

———. *The Thought of Thomas Aquinas*. Oxford: Clarendon, 2009.

Deneen, Patrick. *Why Liberalism Failed*. Princeton: Princeton University Press, 2018.

Dickson, John. *The Best Kept Secret of Christian Mission: Promoting the Gospel with More Than Our Lips*. Grand Rapids: Zondervan, 2010.

Dolan, Jay. *Catholic Revivalism: The American Experience 1830–1900*. South Bend, IN: University of Notre Dame Press, 1978.

Dunn, James. *Romans*. Waco, TX: Thomas Nelson, 1998.

Flechner, Roy. *Saint Patrick Retold*. Princeton: Princeton University Press, 2019.

Galadari, Abdullah. *Qur'anic Hermeneutics*. London: Bloomsbury, 2018.

Garfield, Jay. *Engaging Buddhism: Why it Matters to Philosophy*. Oxford: Oxford University Press, 2014.

Giambrone, Anthony. *A Quest for the Historical Christ*. Washington DC: Catholic University of America Press, 2022.

Gilson, Etienne. *The Christian Philosophy of St. Thomas Aquinas*. Notre Dame: University of Notre Dame Press, 1956.

Gorman, Michael. *The Apostle of the Crucified Lord: A Theological Introduction to Paul and His Letters*. Grand Rapids: Eerdmans, 2017.

Green, Michael. *Evangelism in the Early Church*. Grand Rapids: Eerdmans, 2004.

Habermas, Gary. *On the Resurrection Evidences*. Brentwood, TN: B&H Academic, 2024.

Hahn, Scott. *Evangelizing Catholics: A Mission Manual for the New Evangelization*. Huntington: Our Sunday Visitor, 2014.

Harrison, Victoria. *Eastern Philosophy: The Basics*. London: Routledge, 2012.

Hart, David Bentley. *That All Shall Be Saved: Heaven, Hell, and Universal Salvation*. New Haven: Yale University Press, 2021.

Hsia, R. Po-Chia. *A Jesuit in the Forbidden City: Matteo Ricci*. New York: Oxford University Press, 2012.

House, Adrian. *Saint Francis of Assisi*. Mahwah, NJ: Hidden Spring, 2001.

Irenaeus. *Against the Heresies*. In *A New Eusebius: Documents Illustrating the History of the Church*. Grand Rapids: Baker Academic, 2013.

Jones, Andrew Willard. *The Two Cities: A History of Christian Politics*. Steubenville, OH: Emmaus Road, 2021.

Keith, Chris, and Anthony Le Donne. *Jesus, Criteria, and the Demise of Authenticity*. London: T. & T. Clark, 2012.

Kidd, Thomas. *The Great Awakening: A Brief History with Documents*. Boston: Bedford, 2008.

Kohn, Margaret, and Kavita Reddy. "Colonialism." *Stanford Encyclopedia of Philosophy*. https://plato.stanford.edu/entries/colonialism/.

Krauth, Charles. *The Augsburg Confession of Faith With a Historical Introduction and Notes*. Ithaca, NY: Just and Sinner, 2020.

Lancashire, Ian. *The Homilies*. Toronto: University of Toronto Press, 1994. http://www.anglicanlibrary.org/homilies/bk1homo3.htm.

Lausanne Community for World Evangelization. *The Lausanne Covenant*. https://lausanne.org/content/covenant/lausanne-covenant#cov.

Lebens, Samuel. "Proselytism as Epistemic Violence: A Jewish Approach to the Ethics of Religious Persuasion." *The Monist* 104.3 (2021) 376–92.

Licona, Michael. "Is the Sky Falling in the World of Historical Jesus Research?" *Bulletin for Biblical Research* 26.3 (2016) 353–68.

———. *Resurrection of Jesus: A New Historiographical Approach*. Downers Grove, IL: IVP Academic.

———. *Why Are There Differences in the Gospels?* New York: Oxford University Press, 2016.

MacDonald, Gregory (pseudonym for Robin Parry). *The Evangelical Universalist*. Eugene, OR: Cascade, 2012.

McDowell, Sean. *The Fate of the Apostles*. New York: Routledge, 2016.

McGrath, Alister. *Iustitia Dei: A History of the Christian Doctrine*. Cambridge: Cambridge University Press, 2005.

McIver, Robert. "Collected Memory and the Reliability of the Gospel Tradition." In *Jesus, Skepticism, and the Problem of History: Criteria and Context in the Study of Christian Origins*, edited by Darrell Bock and Robert Komoszewski, 125–44. Grand Rapids: Zondervan, 2019.

McNabb, Tyler Dalton. "Against the Access Requirement: A Plantingian Response to Public Reason Accessibilism." In *The Palgrave Handbook to Religion and State*, edited by Shannon Holzer, 29–40. London: Palgrave MacMillan, 2023.

———. "Analytic Catholic Epistemologies of Faith: A Survey of Developments." *Philosophy Compass* 18/4 (2023). https://compass.onlinelibrary.wiley.com/toc/17479991/2023/18/4.

———. *God and Political Theory*. Cambridge: Cambridge University Press, 2022.

McNabb, Tyler Dalton, and Erik Baldwin. *Classical Theism and Buddhism*. London: Bloomsbury, 2022.

Melanchthon, Philip. *The Apology of the Augsburg Confession: The Trigglotta Edition*. Ithaca, NY: Just and Sinner, 2020.

Moo, Douglas. *The Epistle to the Romans*. Grand Rapids: Eerdmans, 1996.

Moreland, A. "The Qur'an and the doctrine of private revelation." *Theological Studies* 76 (2015) 531–49.

Newman, John. *On Priesthood of Christ in Sermon Notes of John Henry Cardinal Newman 1949–1878*. London: Longmans, Green and Co., 1914.

Newman, John Henry. *Tracts for the Times: Remarks on Certain Passages in the 39 Articles*. http://anglicanhistory.org/tracts/tract90/.

Noonan, John. *A Church that Can and Cannot Change*. South Bend, IN: University of Notre Dame Press, 2005.

O'Collins, Gerald. *A Christology of Religions*. Maryknoll, NY: Orbis, 2018.

O'Collins, Gerald, and Oliver Rafferty. "Roman Catholic View." In *Justification: Five Views*, edited by James Beilby and Paul Eddy, 265–308. Downers Grove, IL: IVP Academic, 2011.

Pascal, Blaise. *Pensées*. London: Penguin, 1995.

Pitre, Brant, Michael Barber, and John Kincaid. *Paul, a New Covenant Jew: Rethinking Pauline Theology*. Grand Rapids: Eerdmans, 2019.

Pope Benedict. *Spe Salvi*. https://www.vatican.va/content/benedict-xvi/en/encyclicals/documents/hf_ben-xvi_enc_20071130_spe-salvi.html.

———. *Wednesday Audience*. November 19, 2008. https://www.vatican.va/content/benedict-xvi/en/audiences/2008/documents/hf_ben-xvi_aud_20081119.html.

BIBLIOGRAPHY

Pope Francis. *Evangelii Gaudium*. https://www.vatican.va/content/francesco/en/apost_exhortations/documents/papa-francesco_esortazione-ap_20131124_evangelii-gaudium.html.

Pope John Paul II. *Evangelium Vitae*. https://www.vatican.va/content/john-paul-ii/en/encyclicals/documents/hf_jp-ii_enc_25031995_evangelium-vitae.html.

———. *Remptoris Missio*. https://www.vatican.va/content/john-paul-ii/en/encyclicals/documents/hf_jp-ii_enc_07121990_redemptoris-missio.html.

Pope Paul VI. *Evangelii Nuntiandi*. https://www.vatican.va/content/paul-vi/en/apost_exhortations/documents/hf_p-vi_exh_19751208_evangelii-nuntiandi.html.

Prothro, James. *A Pauline Theology of Justification: Forgiveness, Friendship, and Life in Christ*. Eugene, OR: Cascade, 2023.

Rambacan, Anantanand. *A Hindu Theology of Liberation*. Albany: State University of New York Press, 2015.

Reynold, Gabriel Said. *The Qur'an and the Bible: Text and Commentary*. New Haven: Yale University Press, 2018.

Rodriguez, Rafael. "Criteria of Embarrassment." In *Jesus, Criteria, and the Demise of Authenticity*, edited by Chris Keith and Anthony Le Donne, 132–51. London: T. & T. Clark, 2012.

Ronholz, Anke. "Crossing the Rubicon: A Historiographical Study." *Mnemosyne* 62 (2009) 432–50.

Śaṁkarācārya. *Shankara's Crest-Jewel of Discrimination*. Translated by Swami Prabhavananda and Christopher Isherwood. Hollywood, CA: Vedānta, 1978.

Sanders, E. P. *Paul: The Apostle's Life, Letters, and Thought*. Minneapolis: Fortress, 2015.

Singer, Peter. "Heavy petting." *Nerve* (2001). www.nerve.com/Opinions/Singer/heavyPetting.

Stanley, Alan, ed. *Four Views on Works at the Final Judgement*. Grand Rapids: Zondervan, 2013.

Stone, Bryan. *Evangelism After Pluralism*. Grand Rapids: Baker Academic, 2018.

Stump, Eleanor. *Aquinas*. Milton Park, UK: Taylor Francis, 2008.

Sullivan, Francis. *Salvation Outside the Church? Tracing the History of the Catholic Response*. Eugene, OR: Wipf and Stock, 2002.

Swinburne, Richard. *Resurrection of God Incarnate*. Oxford: Oxford University Press, 2003.

Thiessen, Elmer. *The Ethics of Evangelism: A Philosophical Defense of Proselytism and Persuasion*. Downers Grove, IL: InterVarsity, 2011.

Tooely, Michael. "Abortion and Infanticide." *Philosophy and Public Affairs* 2.1 (1972) 37–65.

Unger, Peter. "A Defense of Skepticism." *The Philosophical Review* (1971) 198–210.

Vallier, Kevin. *All Kingdoms of the World*. New York: Oxford University Press, 2023.

———. "Convergence and Consensus." *Public Affairs Quarterly* (2011) 261–80

———. *Liberal Politics and Public Faith: Beyond Separation*. London: Routledge, 2014.

Wallace, Daniel. "Textual Criticism and the Criterion of Embarrassment." In *Jesus, Skepticism, and the Problem of History: Criteria and Context in the Study of Christian Origins*, edited by Darrell Bock and Robert Komoszewski, 93–124. Grand Rapids: Zondervan, 2019.

Walsh, Leo. "Proselytism and Evangelization: Important Distinctions for Catholic Catechists." https://www.usccb.org/beliefs-and-teachings/how-we-teach/catechesis/catechetical-sunday/new-evangelization/upload/Fr-Walsh-Proselytism-and-Evangelization.pdf.

Ward, Keith. *Religion and Revelation*. Oxford: Oxford University Press, 1994.

Wax, Trevin. "The Justification Debate: A Primer." *Christianity Today* 53.6 (2009) 34–35.

The Westminster Divines. *The Westminster Confession of Faith*. Sydney South: Christian Education and Publications, 2007.

Wright, N. T. *Justification: God's Plan and Paul's Vision*. Downers Grove: IVP Academic, 2009.

———. *Paul and the Faithfulness of God*. Minneapolis: Fortress, 2013.

www.ingramcontent.com/pod-product-compliance
Lightning Source LLC
Chambersburg PA
CBHW020207090426
42734CB00008B/975